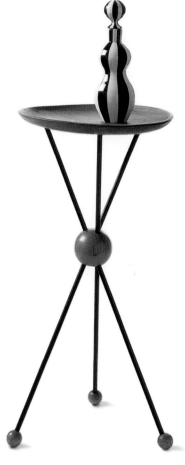

The
DOMAIN
BOOK
of Intuitive
Home Design

The DOMAIN BOOK

of Intuitive Home Design

HOW TO DECORATE USING YOUR PERSONALITY TYPE

JUDY GEORGE WITH TODD LYON

Principle Photography by Steven Randazzo

Design by Stark Design Associates

CLARKSON POTTER/PUBLISHERS

NEW YORK

Published by Clarkson N. Potter, Inc., 201 East 50th Street, New York, New York 10022. Member of
the Crown Publishing Group.

Random House, Inc. New York, Toronto, London, Sydney, Auckland
www.randomhouse.com

CLARKSON N. POTTER, POTTER, and colophon are trademarks of Clarkson N. Potter, Inc.

Printed in China

Library of Congress Cataloging-in-Publication Data
George, Judy.
    The Domain book of intuitive home design / Judy George with Todd Lyon. — 1st ed.
1. Interior decoration—Psychological aspects. I. Lyon, Todd. II. Title.
NK2113.G46   1998
747—dc21   97-46874

ISBN 0-517-70763-2

10 9 8 7 6 5 4 3 2 1

First Edition

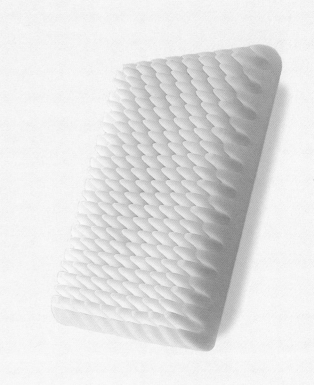

Contents

What is style?

Is it an ability to put things together in an attractive manner?

Is it a well-developed sense of aesthetics?

Is it a talent for anticipating trends?

No. These are merely the end products of something much larger and more significant.

Style is *yearning.*

It is the human impulse to create shapes, colors, tones, and textures that tell the truth about who we are. It is the instinct to make a home—that one maddening, beautiful place where we belong. It is an

ongoing, lifelong search for what *feels* completely right.

Home is much more than a safe harbor that shelters us from weather and darkness; it is our particular place in the universe. Though we may concern ourselves with the news of the world, the business of business, or the art of art, the fact of home is in our bones. In times of war, entire countries rise up to defend their home-

lands. Home is as powerful as—and often inseparable from—religion and love.

In our culture, one of the most significant rites of passage is the separation from our parents' home and the making of a place to call our own. It may be a shack at the edge of the sea, a condo in a small town, a flat in an urban neighborhood, or a grand house on a

green hill. But no matter what it looks like, the creation of our home begins as a declaration of independence and evolves into an expression of self that's as distinctive as a fingerprint, a scent, a voice, a face. From a vast jumble of options we select our location, our building, our furniture, our equipment, our palettes, lighting, surfaces, systems, and decorative touches. Often these choices are heavily tempered by circumstances and shaped by outside influences, but what ultimately assembles around us is a life that looks like us.

Our choices don't come out of nowhere. A flamboyant woman who speaks in fiery phrases and sketches pictures in the air would be unlikely to live in a spartan flat furnished with a cot and a straight-backed chair. Likewise, a plain-talking man who abhors artifice and loves the feeling of honest dirt under his fingers would hardly set himself up in a posh penthouse with velvet drapes and gold-leaf flourishes. Whether it's plain, fancy, offhand, or deliberate, our sense of style is always a reflection of our history, our temperament, our impulses—in short, it is a reflection of our personality. Successful self-expression begins with an understanding of one's self, and understanding one's self is what this book is all about.

The Domain Book of Intuitive Home Design is the first book to identify and define the connection between personality and style. It groups people into four general categories: the Visionary, the Artisan, the Idealist, and the Adventurer. Beginning with a personality quiz, this book leads the reader on a very personal journey in which one's aesthetic choices are linked

to childhood circumstances, deeply rooted tendencies, and native talents. Along the way it answers such questions as: Why do some people insist on neat, tidy rooms, while other people tend to pile their stuff all over tables, chairs, and floors? Why do some folks crave airy rooms with curtainless windows, while others are more comfortable in cozy quarters with cushions and drapery all around? This book explains why Adventurers tend to have the best party houses; why Visionaries' homes promote solitude and reflection; why family reunions are most likely to happen at Artisans' homes; and how Idealists' homes manage to blend high style and low maintenance.

The following pages are filled with home decorating ideas and images, but this book's goal is not simply to provide inspiration. It also seeks to promote understanding of ourselves and others. It seeks to uncover the meaning of personal aesthetics and, ultimately, to empower readers to create home environments that cradle their true selves.

I hope you will recognize yourself and your loved ones in this book. I hope

that, upon learning the four basic intuitive types, you can listen more sympathetically to the needs of your body, mind, spirit, and sense of humor. I hope that the Intuitive System will challenge you, entertain you, and enrich your life; especially, I hope that this book helps you discover your honest, authentic home, the one place that feels exactly right for you.

The Quiz

Taking the Quiz

At the heart of the Intuitive Design System is the following twenty-question quiz. There are no right or wrong answers; in fact, the quiz is really a selection of preferences, and completing it should be as easy and pleasurable as ordering favorite dishes from a menu. There are some guidelines, however.

When taking the quiz, pretend that you live in a world without financial hardship or compromised circumstances. Follow your inner fantasies, not your real-life needs. For instance, if asked about your ideal vacation home, choose a place that captures your fancy; don't consider what your mate or your family might prefer, or where you can afford to travel this year.

Try to be flexible and place yourself within the scenario that the question suggests. For example, if a question asks you to give up one household appliance out of several, you should imagine that you already own all the appliances listed. Some of the questions will place you within traditional jobs and steady relationships; if these circumstances don't apply to you, do your best to picture yourself within those circumstances and respond accordingly.

In most of the following questions, you will be asked to choose one answer out of four. Some questions have eight answers; of these, you may choose either one or two. Please read each question carefully.

Though the quiz is most accurate when each question is completed according to instructions, you might come across a question in which *none* of the answers seems at all right for you. If this should happen, simply skip it and move on to the next question.

Conversely, if you find a question in which you're hopelessly torn between two answers, you may choose them both.

The Intuitive Personality Quiz

1. You're about to hit a personal milestone (major birthday, anniversary, etc.) and have learned that a close friend is throwing a surprise party for you. In your secret heart, you hope the upcoming event is:

    a .... An elegant affair at a fine restaurant or hotel

    b .... An all-night bash with music and dancing

    c .... A high-spirited outdoor party, with picnicking, swimming, skating, or similar activity

    d .... A lively gathering built around an event, such as a concert, ball game, or other spectacle

2. While attending a lecture, you note that the speaker has made a statement which you are quite sure is inaccurate. The lecture is followed by a question-and-answer session. Your response is to:

    a .... Say nothing, but later mail a diplomatic note to the speaker questioning his or her statement.

    b .... Introduce yourself to the speaker after the lecture, and discuss the issue in person.

    c .... Discuss the issue with friends, but don't bring it to the attention of the speaker.

    d .... Bring up the issue during the question-and-answer session.

3. You're celebrating Thanksgiving with a large gathering of friends and/or family. Everybody is pitching in to make the evening a success. Which *two* of the following jobs would you most enjoy doing?

    a .... Creating the table settings

    b .... Planning the music

    c .... Preparing food

    d .... Building the fire

    e .... Carving the turkey

    f .... Selecting a Thanksgiving prayer or toast

    g .... Keeping the kids entertained

    h .... Organizing after-dinner games

4. While shopping, you try on a terrific outfit that suits you perfectly but is out of your price range. Your reaction is to:

       a .... Give yourself a few days to think about it, then buy it if it still seems like what you want.

       b .... Buy it and decide later whether to return it or not.

       c .... Find out when it's going to go on sale, then take your chances that it will still be there.

       d .... Just say no.

5. Of the following romantic gifts, which would you find most pleasurable to give or receive?

       a .... A dozen long-stemmed roses

       b .... A balloon ride for two

       c .... A professionally photographed portrait of you, your loved one, or your family

       d .... An engraved Rolex

6. In a poker game, you bet and lose one household appliance. Which of the following do you sacrifice?

       a .... The microwave oven

       b .... The home security system

       c .... The cellular phone

       d .... The camcorder

7. You're at the end of a particularly stressful workday. Which of the following restorative scenarios sounds most appealing to you? (Choose only one.)

       a .... An evening alone with new videos, books, and/or magazines

       b .... A rendezvous with friends at a pub, club, or coffeehouse

       c .... An afternoon puttering in the garden

       d .... An uninterrupted night of good TV

       e .... A workout at the gym followed by a sauna, steam bath, or whirlpool

       f .... A fragrant soak in the tub with a good novel

       g .... A leisurely walk or bike ride

       h .... A long motorcycle ride

8. A genie pops out of a bottle and offers you two wishes, but there's a hitch: You can only ask for items that will benefit you personally, and they have to be chosen from his preapproved wish list. Which *two* do you choose?

a .... Inner peace

b .... Energy

c .... Harmony

d .... Justice

e .... Security

f .... Beauty

g .... Wellness

h .... Creativity

9. On the job, you're assigned to a new, entirely experimental project. How do you approach the task?

a .... Read books, articles, and other materials relating to the project, then proceed with your own innovative plan.

b .... Go headlong into the project, seeking out information as it's needed.

c .... Seek out an experienced person to act as a teacher, and consult this person through each phase of the project.

d .... Learn all you can about the subject, devise a plan, and propose it to your employers before proceeding.

10. You've won a fantasy vacation to a fabulous, far-off land. The prize includes various lodging options. Which *one* place do you choose as your temporary home away from home?

a .... A suite in an elegant "little" hotel in the center of town with excellent room service

b .... A houseboat docked at a lively waterfront

c .... A spacious cottage on the beach

d .... A suite in a modern, big-city luxury hotel

e .... A well-appointed set of rooms at a private country club

f .... An old-world villa

g .... A farmhouse surrounded by orchards

h .... A room in the home of an eccentric millionaire

11. You've had a run-in with the law. Lucky for you, a sympathetic judge has allowed you to choose your own sentence from the following options. How do you repay your debt to society?

a .... Make recordings for the blind every Sunday for a year.

b .... Give motivational speeches to juvenile offenders.

c .... Take in a foster child for six weeks.

d .... Pay a fee equal to 10 percent of your annual salary.

12. You're showing your home to a new friend. He or she admiringly picks up an item from the mantelpiece and accidentally drops it. It breaks. What happens next?

a .... You're gracious about the accident, but are secretly dismayed that your guest would handle your possessions without asking.

b .... You're entirely forgiving and do your best to inject humor into the moment.

c .... You put the loss out of your mind and concentrate on putting your embarrassed guest at ease.

d .... Though you behave diplomatically, you resent the uncomfortable position the incident has put you in.

13. Your accountant has informed you that you must choose a charity from the following list. Which *one* do you pick?

a .... The National Endowment for the Arts

b .... Big Brother/Big Sister

c .... Greenpeace

d .... Amnesty International

e .... United Way

f .... National Public Radio

g .... Habitat for Humanity

h .... Act Up

14. Your love relationship has taken a turn for the worse; your mate has begun to act strangely. Of the following behaviors, which would be the *most* difficult for you to handle?

a .... Your mate starts to spend every day lying on the sofa, watching TV.

b .... He or she starts imposing rigid household rules about schedules, chores, budgets, etc.

c .... He or she spends increasing amounts of time away from home, with little explanation.

      d .... Your mate stops participating in household tasks, leaving you with all the cleaning, cooking, shopping, and bill paying.

15. A close friend has organized a silent auction for charity; you are obligated to join in. Which of the following *two* items do you bid on?

      a .... An eighteenth-century portrait

      b .... An Alaskan cruise

      c .... A greenhouse

      d .... A 1966 Mustang convertible

      e .... A video phone

      f .... A Persian carpet

      g ...... An antique trundle bed

      h .... Dinner for six at a new, highly regarded restaurant

16. Your assistant performs his or her job brilliantly, except for one problem that so irks you you're considering looking for a replacement. What is it?

      a .... Your assistant, in spite of a reasonably good education, has shockingly poor grammar and spelling.

      b .... You sense that your assistant, while always reliable and attentive, is secretly bucking for your job.

      c .... Your assistant is entirely undemonstrative, to the extent that even a generous Christmas bonus doesn't warrant a thank you.

      d .... Although your assistant always comes through when it matters, he or she is often late, has a messy desk, and keeps a haphazard filing system.

17. You have inherited an old house and are preparing to move in. It has a room that's too small to be a bedroom. You decide to convert it into:

      a .... A cedar-lined closet for storing clothing, linens, etc.

      b .... A dressing room

      c .... A creative studio (wood shop, sewing room, music room, etc.)

      d .... A gym

18. Fate has taken you to a lovely spa where you are allowed to choose a free treatment from the following list. What's your pleasure?

      a .... A haircut and a facial

      b .... A full-body acupressure treatment

      c .... An herbal wrap followed by a swim in the hot springs

      d .... A complete fitness analysis

19. While taking a Sunday drive down country lanes, you come upon a cross-roads with four signs pointing in four directions. Which do you follow?

      a .... "Elderly sisters selling house full of antiques. Go one mile, look for Tudor mansion."

      b .... "Grand Opening: Amazing Maze of Hedges. Be the first to reach the center of the maze, win $5,000."

      c .... "This way to Abby's Magical Herb Garden . . . free consultation with highly reputable witch."

      d .... "Convention of dreamers and inventors now underway. Public welcome. Follow signs to geodesic dome."

20. Your hefty retirement fund has finally paid off, and you can now choose a home in which to really *live*—presumably for the rest of your life. Which *one* of the following options attracts you most?

      a .... A renovated brownstone on a leafy city block

      b .... A Gothic cathedral in the middle of the city

      c .... A rambling country house on a pond

      d .... A luxury condominium in a resort area

      e .... A modern beach house with a full glass wall overlooking the surf

      f .... A former sea captain's house with manicured lawns and a view of the ocean

      g .... A ranch, complete with outbuildings and 200 acres of land

      h .... A gutted factory with a certificate of occupancy

Scoring

On the following list, make a hatch mark next to each corresponding answer (that is, every time you've answered "B" or "H" on the test, make a hatch mark next to "B & H").

    A & F =

    B & H =

    C & G =

    D & E =

Add up the total number of hatch marks in each category.

Results

If most of your answers were ...... then you are most like:

<u>A & F</u>—a VISIONARY.

<u>B & H</u>—an ADVENTURER.

<u>C & G</u>—an ARTISAN.

<u>D & E</u>—an IDEALIST.

Interpreting the Quiz

Intuitive Design is based on four archetypal personalities: the Visionary, the Artisan, the Idealist, and the Adventurer. These personality types are broadly drawn categories that describe and define certain human tendencies. But since it's impossible for living, breathing individuals to be poured into predesigned molds, it follows that virtually no individual will fit neatly into a single archetype. Upon completing the quiz, most people find that their answers have spilled into all categories, with one or two types ultimately dominating the rest.

In determining the quiz results, logic rules. If you, for instance, have nineteen hatches next to "A&F" and only a few answers in other categories, then you have extremely strong Visionary tendencies. If most of your answers fall into two categories, then you're probably a hybrid of those two types and will most likely feel allied with both. It's not unusual, however, for an individual's answers to be almost evenly scattered between three or four categories: this simply means that you have a broad range of impulses and tendencies, and various facets of your character are sympathetic with various types.

Using the Book

The first section of *The Domain Book of Intuitive Home Design* describes and analyzes the four archetypes. The second section is a "house tour" that shows, room by room, how the four archetypes express themselves in their home environments.

As you begin to learn more about the archetypes and see how style is a reflection of personality, you may end up claiming an entirely different type for yourself—even if it contradicts your quiz results. That's okay, too. After all, this is a book about self-discovery and, ultimately, a better understanding of your own personal expression. For more information, go to www.intuitive-home.com

Intuitive Archetypes

What Do You Do with a

Naked

Sofa?

There it sits, plumped and perfect, freshly delivered to your living room. Your new sofa. Virginal as its pristine sister on the showroom floor, and just as pretty.

Now comes the challenge: how do you make it your own? Well, that all depends on your personality. If you're a **Visionary**, you'll want to flank it with matching tables, pad it with tapestry pillows, and slip an Oriental rug beneath it. If you're an **Artisan**, you'll think first of comfort: Will an ottoman make the setup cozier? How about an afghan, a reading lamp, a coffee table with a fragrant bowl of flowers? An **Idealist** will think like an architect and keep the setup clean and dramatic. If the sofa's long and low, the Idealist will counterbalance it with a strong vertical element and keep the room open, with no fussy details to distract the eye. The **Adventurer,** on the other hand, will make the sofa into a personal statement. Draped with leopard-print throws or scattered with tiny purple pillows, it will appear to have been created not in a factory but in its owner's imagination.

In the hands of the Visionary, the Artisan, the Idealist, and the Adventurer, one sofa will take on four entirely different looks. It will become a reflection of its owner's yearnings; in fact, it will become an extension of its owner's personality.

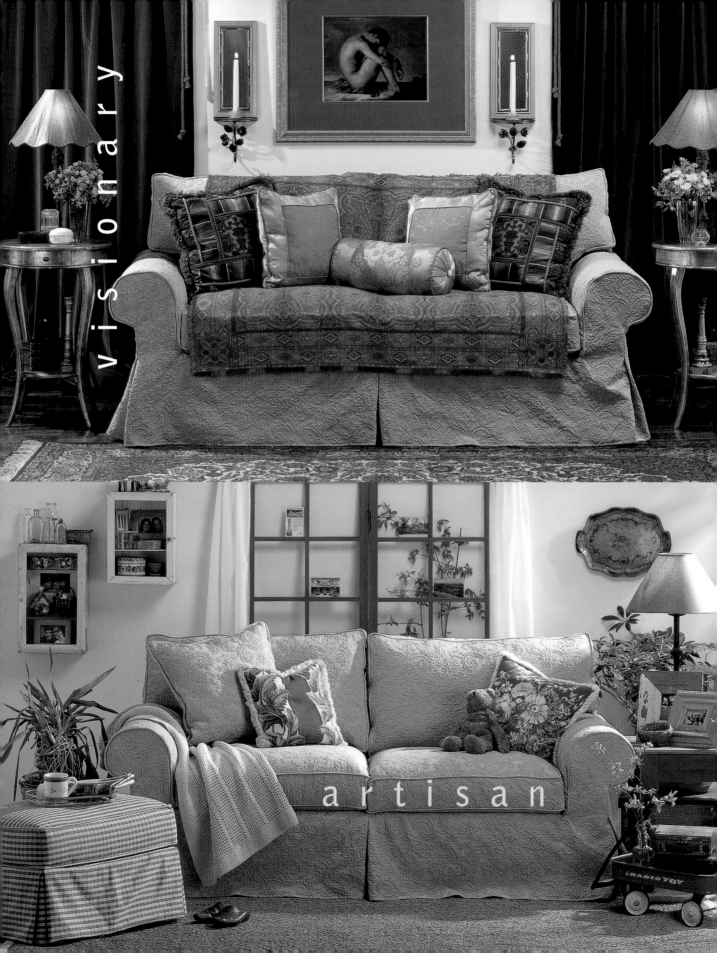

visionary

artisan

idealist

adventurer

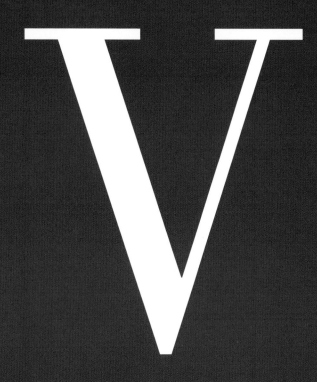

V

When you have shut your doors and darkened your room, remember never to say that

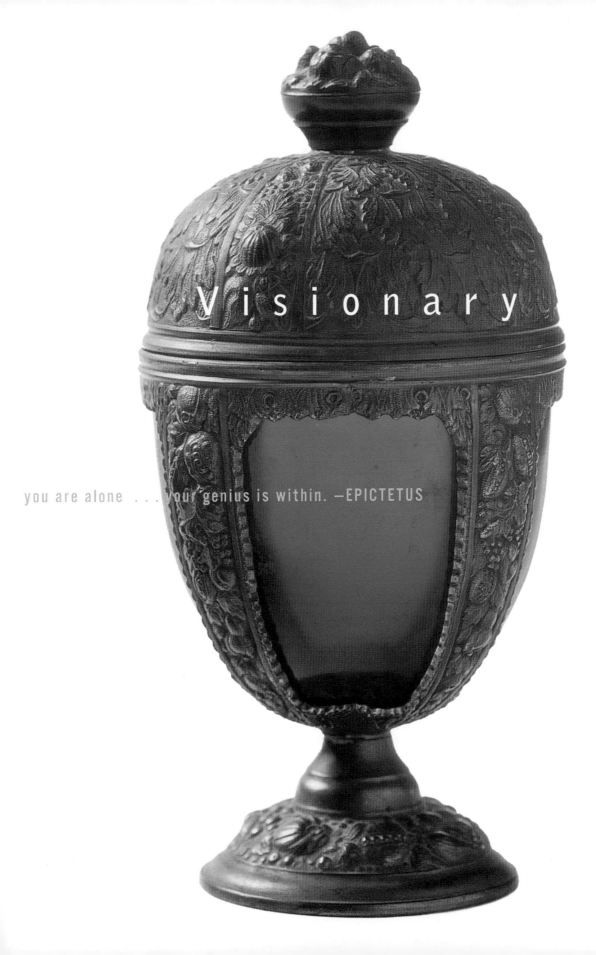

Visionary

you are alone . . . your genius is within. —EPICTETUS

IN A PERFECT WORLD, each Visionary would have a private sanctuary. Furnishings and accessories would be unique; lighting would be kind; walls of bookshelves would be filled with inspiring volumes; lovely things would be everywhere.

To the Visionary, any other setting would Civilized be a compromise. This is not because Visionaries need to impress people; on the contrary, Visionaries often seek to escape other people. Though they may function extremely well in the outside world and achieve high levels of success, the everyday clatter and stress of daily life make the Visionary feel exhausted and ungrounded. And home is where the Visionary goes to become centered again. The deep carpets, the soft sofa, the hot bath, the reliable routines of home—these function as a kind of self-affirmation. Surrounded by what is familiar, beloved, and beautiful, Visionaries can remember themselves and find their place in the world. Home is safety and sanity, a place to breathe deeply and easily. It is the Visionary's favorite destination.

Inside the Visionary's Head

Visionaries are highly evolved creatures. There is nothing simple about them; they are entire cultures unto themselves. Within the Visionary dwell a judge and jury, an impetuous spirit and a stern censor, an empathic soul who feels the world's sorrows, and a blistering critic who cannot accept its sloppy faults.

Similar things could be said of other types. But Visionaries are blessed and cursed by an intense ability to Reverent see. Their analytical skills are so acute that they can often recognize problems and solutions at a glance; they tend to have an innate understanding of art, music and literature; and they are often so perceptive that they can literally feel other people's pain, joy, and anxiety.

What most Visionaries do not have is a good filtering system. They cannot turn their receptors on and off at will, and they lack a natural ability to block out unwanted stimuli. Hectic work environments, overbearing people, raucous gatherings, the dog barking upstairs—such distractions can overwhelm Visionaries.

PRIVATE

Without art, the crudeness of reality would make the world unbearable. —GEORGE BERNARD SHAW

Intense

Independent

Passionate

The Italian novelist Italo Calvino once wrote about a man who confused himself with things outside himself. When the man ate soup, for instance, he thought he *was* soup, and the world became "nothing but a vast shapeless mass of soup in which all things dissolved."

Yes, Calvino was something of a surrealist. But Visionaries, while they may not confuse themselves with soup, can be said to have unusually fluid ego boundaries. On the plus side, this gives them a great capacity for suspension of disbelief, which means they can blissfully lose themselves in novels and movies—

You May Be a Visionary If . . .

- You dislike purple but are rather fond of aubergine.
- You'd rather have a terrace than a porch.
- You adore your ancestors but could do without your relatives.
- You consider cheap paperbacks disposable but hang on to high-end design and literary magazines.
- You refuse to put an unattractive gift on display even when the person who gave it to you comes to visit.
- You like the concept of democracy, but you aren't sure about people wearing sweat suits to casinos.
- You're attracted to shiny things.
- You avoid buying exercise equipment because you don't have a good place to hide it.
- You always ask the hotel chambermaid to bring extra towels.
- You can use the word "toile" in a sentence.
- You yearn for the days of the grand ocean liners.
- You are determined to go to Ascot just once before you die.
- You're delighted to receive flowers unexpectedly—unless the arrangement is mostly mums and carnations.
- You have your piano tuned twice a year, even though nobody has played it since 1972.
- You have more than four pillows on your bed.
- You know what putti are.
- You keep sachets in your drawers.
- You could easily spend eight months searching for the right sofa.
- Your monthly dry-cleaning bill is roughly equal to your monthly utility bill.
- You keep your good jewelry separate from your costume jewelry.
- Your luggage matches.
- Your house has a name.
- All of your favorite artists are dead.
- You love antique furniture, but you would never wear secondhand clothes.
- You keep separate stemware for red wine, white wine, martinis, margaritas, cordials, cognac, and champagne.
- You don't like opening mail without a letter opener.
- Your idea of natural childbirth is no makeup.
- When you open the drapes in the living room you see . . . curtains.
- You do not own a baseball cap.
- You do the crossword puzzle not only in ink but with a fountain pen.

A good marriage is that in which each appoints the other the guardian of his solitude.

—RAINER MARIA RILKE

unless someone's talking during the film. The downside is that they can also lose their sense of perspective and, along with it, their sense of humor.

In order to protect themselves, Visionaries create artificial boundaries between themselves and others. The person who wears a Walkman on the subway is probably a Visionary. So is the office mate who goes directly home at five o'clock every day. The neighbor who chats over the fence but never opens the gate, the co-worker who declines to join the car pool, the friend who takes the phone off the hook—these Visionaries are establishing boundaries so that they can secure precious time alone.

And private time is what Visionaries need. When they are alone, protected from the chaos and din of day-to-day life, Visionaries come back to themselves and feel whole.

The Eye of the Storm

All human beings need to find their own safe place in the world. Artisans find peace in the rhythms of nature and the security of family; Idealists depend on reliable systems outside themselves; Adventurers seek constant stimuli to remind them that they are alive and vital. But Visionaries take a very different path: they seek a place within themselves that is utterly their own, that will not be invaded, diluted, distorted, or tainted by the influences of the outside world.

It is this sacred, mythic self that defines the Visionary. Some get in touch with it through religion or prayer, others through the creation of art; usually, though, Visionaries can feel safe, quiet, and centered simply by going home. Surrounded by what is familiar and beloved, the Visionary remembers: This is

who I am. This painting of my grandfather, this cabinet filled with teacups and saucers, this armchair by the fireside: I am these things, and they are me.

Because home is their sanctuary, Visionaries are exceedingly cautious about who—and what—they let in. Few things are more painful to Visionaries than having to share space with people they don't love. The college roommate who draws a chalk line down the center of the dorm room is almost certainly a Visionary. Though that line may be, to a certain extent, drawn in protest against the roommate's messiness or habits, more likely it is the Visionary's way of mapping out his or her private territory.

A Laser-Beam Intelligence

William Blake once wrote of a desire to "see a world in a grain of sand." If anyone can be said to have that gift, it is the Visionary. When confronted with problems, Visionaries do not run around gathering data and opinions. Rather, they sit down and think. Visionaries have a Zen-like ability to meditate and concentrate until answers reveal themselves; they learn by becoming one with their subject.

This may sound like heady stuff, but it's how poets, painters, and designers routinely do their work. It is a process of understanding that doesn't rely on empirical information; in fact, Visionaries suffer when they're given too much factual material. To function at their best they need a narrow, specific focus. Then they can shine their empathic light through a magnifying glass of intellect, and all things may be revealed.

This laser-beam intelligence is wondrous, but it can be a real drag at parties. Because they concentrate intensely on one thing at a time, small talk can be downright painful to Visionaries. A stranger's cheerful chatter, lacking direction and meaning, may come at them like a swarm of bees. Though intended as a social nicety, random small talk can prompt Visionaries to eyeball the exits and search for some gracious excuse to leave.

This is not to say that Visionaries can't be charming, amusing, and engaging. Many are. But they prefer socializing one-on-one, and they crave situations in which they don't have to dull themselves or mute their opinions in order to fit in.

Though Visionaries are most relaxed when they're at home alone or with a select companion, it's great fun for them to go head-to-head with someone who can match their intensity.

The Heart of the Visionary

Although Visionaries are not exactly loners, they would rather have one close friend than a herd of acquaintances. They also tend to have fiercely monogamous and totally passionate love relationships. These communions are built on a trust so complete that it borders on the holy.

In order for a Visionary to have true intimacy with another, a kind of fusing must take place. In those rare, significant instances when a person is invited to cross over to the Visionary's private, inner sanctum, the result is a "you and me against the world" dynamic. To the Visionary, such a relationship is an extremely serious commitment. The Visionary becomes one with another, in friendship or in love, and this union is expected to last a lifetime.

Where love exists, Visionaries can be infinitely forgiving of others' quirks and habits. One heart, one hand, one sofa: home becomes a sanctuary for two instead of one.

Even in the best matches, however, Visionaries cherish their privacy. Double rooms in hotels are the Visionaries' idea of heaven: they can be close to the one they love while still having their very own king-size bed on which to spread maps and magazines. When Katharine Hepburn said men and women should live next door to each other "and just visit now and then," she undoubtedly won the hearts of Visionaries everywhere.

HOUSE-HUNTING WITH THE VISIONARY

Look for:

Manors

Châteaux

Tudor-style homes

Vintage Colonials facing the sea or a well-manicured village green

New York brownstones

Prewar duplexes

Anything Baroque, Georgian, Regency, Empire, Victorian, Edwardian, or Beaux Arts

A suite of rooms at the Plaza

Avoid:

Walk-up apartments

Railroad flats

Houses with prominent garages

Handyman specials

Anything rustic

Homes with vinyl or aluminum siding

Structures built after 1939

Shares

Inside the Visionary's Home

Visitors to a Visionary's home may feel as though they've entered an intimate museum, a human-scale temple of personal expression. It is not only the fascinating furnishings and effects that cause this feeling; it is the fact that Visionaries intuitively build altars. These are not religious shrines (in most cases); rather they are balanced symmetrical compositions. The Visionary will instinctively locate the aesthetic center of a room—an arched window, a fireplace, French doors—and treat it as a visual icon around which to arrange seating and side pieces. If a room lacks an obvious focal point, Visionaries will be compelled to create one. This may be a dramatic work of art or perhaps an ever-replenished flower arrangement. A dining room will seem empty to a Visionary unless there's a chandelier or a centerpiece.

The Visionary's love of divine balance can be expressed in many ways. He or she might artfully create place settings to enhance the beauty of a plate, or perhaps dress a tall window with lace and drapery to make a soft shrine.

Though Visionaries sometimes create altars from unexpected objects, the most important object will hold its place of honor in the center. The result is not only lovely but symbolic as well: the centerpiece represents the Visionary in a safe and supported place of belonging. In fact, it represents the Visionary at home.

Timelessness Is on My Side

Visionaries favor period decor and European-style furnishings. Yet they are rarely purists (that's the Idealist's job), and will fearlessly group traditional pieces with unique or even eccentric elements plucked from any old era or culture.

Though the Visionary style may allude to times gone by, Visionaries themselves do not live in the past. Unlike Artisans, who have a genuine aversion to new things, Visionaries are all for conveniences such as new appliances, central air conditioning,

Elegance is good taste plus a dash of daring.—CARMEL WHITE SNOW

and up-to-date plumbing. They are put off by the stripped-down utilitarian look of modern appliances and fixtures, however, and so they conceal them. Or, if they can't conceal them, they disguise them.

In the Visionary kitchen one may have trouble at first locating the refrigerator and dishwasher; that's because they're probably camouflaged as cabinets. The countertop in a Visionary bathroom may be a Regency-style writing table in which a sink has been discreetly installed, while a brand-new Jacuzzi might sport faucets that look as though they once graced an English manor house. Visionaries have a talent for making every room in the house feel like a turn-of-the-century parlor.

Another way that Visionaries soften the edges of the modern world is by draping. Visionaries find the fluidity of fabric seductive, and many will unabashedly swathe, cloak, swag, or veil everything from tables to walls. Give them fringe on the lampshades, dust ruffles on the beds, and fat tassels dripping off the arms of sofas; these plush touches swaddle the Visionary in luxury.

The Secret Life of Frames

In the Visionary home, frames are everywhere. There are the obvious frames that enclose works of art, and then there are the frames that encircle rooms, such as crown molding around ceilings and baseboards around floors. Within these large frames one might notice elegant paneling with raised borders, or windows with ornamental architraves. If a home wasn't originally graced with such architectural details, a true Visionary will find a way to add them.

The Visionaries' penchant for framing can be traced to their strong desire to tame chaos. They find no joy in rangy, ill-defined spaces. Unlike Adventurers, to whom vast raw lofts are the most exciting spaces imaginable, Visionaries are most comfortable in intimate settings. They like to be contained; they want their spaces to have a focus and structure.

It isn't surprising that picture frames in Visionary homes are sometimes more precious than the images they surround. Many a Visionary would rather have a mediocre oil painting, beautifully framed and displayed, than a decent print unframed and tacked to a wall.

Shhh

Home is where the Visionary's mental health is, and they need surroundings that promote tranquillity: Carpeting, draperies, and doors that close firmly are de rigueur. More obscure aspects of quietude, however, involve color, texture, and materials. Visionaries subconsciously surround themselves with hushed surfaces; they layer their rooms with napped fabrics while avoiding loud design choices like solid primary colors, strong tonal contrasts, and unbroken expanses of glass, marble, or metal.

Quiet lighting, too, is essential. Dimmer switches can be a Visionary's best friend, but even when empowered to brighten or lower lights at will, Visionaries often choose well-shaded table lamps, floor lamps, and oodles of candles.

When home life is disrupted by, say, ongoing construction, a blaring television set, or bickering relatives, Visionaries can feel as though they are falling apart. That's when they bow out and escape into a private mini-environment. In a steamy bathroom they'll sink into bubbles and get lost in a novel. Or, on a bed piled with pillows, they'll scribble in a diary or flip through the pages of a magazine. Every Visionary needs what Virginia Woolf needed: a room of one's own. To the Visionary, solitude means survival.

Look, Don't Touch

One hallmark of the Visionary home is its special areas that are meant to be seen but not touched. It is a very Visionary choice, for instance, to place keepsakes in a glass-front display case where they can be admired but not handled.

Visionaries have a genuine need to keep certain precious possessions out of reach. They like owning two sets of dishes—one for daily use and one for fancier affairs—and will often set things aside to save for special occasions. Quite often, in fact, a Visionary will own something so very special that it never gets used. A collection of silverware owned by a grandmother or a set of bone china handed down by an aunt may be forever locked in a mahogany cabinet, taken out only for periodic cleanings. Such an arrangement sits comfortably with Visionaries: they're suited to the role of curator. In fact, the ritual of polishing Grammy's silverware may be far more meaningful—and much less anxiety-provoking—than bringing it out for dinner parties.

The inclination to segregate possessions is an expression of the Visionary's need for strong borders. That same impulse can be seen in the Visionary's fondness for use-specific rooms. Visionaries adore old houses that have highly specialized rooms such as solariums, nurseries, conservatories, and libraries. They work hard to maintain the sanctity of spaces; the dining room, for instance, is not used for paperwork, and one does not eat supper while sitting on the sofa.

Extreme Visionaries can be almost maniacal about keeping sacred spaces in the home, to the point where certain rooms are impeccably decorated and virtually never used. So where does the Visionary really live? Most likely he or she retreats to a cozy nest in some corner of the house where there's a comfy sofa and a door that closes.

Pockets of Perfection

A home doesn't reflect only its owner's tastes; it also reflects its owner's priorities. Circumstances might cause a Visionary's home to be a wreck, temporarily or permanently, but a Visionary is still a Visionary and will therefore maintain some kind of special place where beauty and harmony reign, even if that place is virtually invisible. Perhaps the Visionary writes exquisite letters in a fine hand, or maintains a checkbook that is balanced to the penny. Though certainly less obvious than owning a home worthy of *Architectural Digest*, these pockets of perfection, held fast against the chaos of life, can sustain and center the Visionary.

The Visionary Alphabet

antiques • art books • atriums • balconies • bas-reliefs • Beaux Arts • bone china • book templates • breakfronts • brownstones • busts • Camelot • candelabra • canopy beds • caryatids • cathedrals • centerpieces • chair rails • chandeliers • china cabinets • chinoiserie • Chippendale • club chairs • coats of arms • columns • crystal • dadoes • door knockers • drapery • ecru • egg-and-dart patterns • Empire • engraved stationery • Fabergé eggs • fainting couches • figurative art • fireplace screens • fountain pens • frames • friezes • French Provincial • fringe • gilt • gold • grand pianos • heirlooms • Italian tile • ivy • jewels • jib doors • kilims • keepsakes • lace • lawns • leather-bound books • libraries • linens • mahogany • mansions • marble • mirrors • murals • neoclassical art • old leather • opera glasses • Oriental carpets • ottomans • paintings • peonies • place cards • porcelain • portraits • precious metals • private elevators • quill pens • quarry stone • raw silk • Regency • rococo • roses • sachets • sconces • silver services • slipper chairs • sterling silver • swags • table carpets • table runners • tapestry • tassels • tea sets • terraces • thrones • tortoiseshell • town houses • trompe l'oeil • Tudor • umbrella stands • upholstery • vanities • vases • velvet • Versailles • widow's walks • window scarves • wine cellars • yule logs • zoning laws

a

All decorating is about memories. —SISTER PARISH

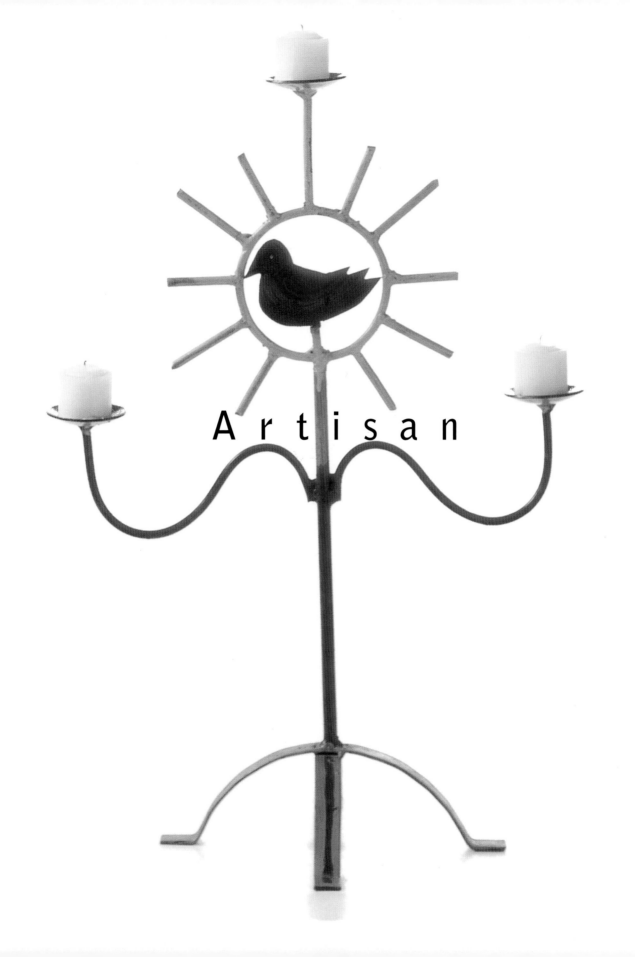

Artisan

DEEP AS THE OCEAN. Lighter than air. Warm as the summer winds. Constant as the North Star. These overused expressions take on new meaning when applied to the Artisan because they are, in so many ways, true.

Artisans aren't apt to draw attention to themselves. In manner they are low-key, pleasant, modest. So you may not notice at first that Artisans are those essential people around whom entire civilizations seem to blossom. You can see them in cities, rescuing buildings from neglect or lending a hand to those in need. In the country you can find them renovating abandoned farmhouses or tilling and tending gardens. In communities large and small Artisans breathe life into what might otherwise have been lost; they nurture growth and cultivate hope.

The Artisan's natural place is at the center of a family—even if that family consists of friends, neighbors, or a half dozen stray cats. It is the Artisan who can be counted on to hold the group together; the Artisan is the cornerstone, the steadfast keeper of promises who lays down day-to-day rhythms so that others may dance in time.

Artisans strive for a life of simplicity, and they don't depend on material things to make them happy. Though they may love shopping, decorating, and collecting, they can, if necessary, get along with very little. Earth, air, fire, and water can be nearly enough for them; add love and the picture is complete.

Inside the Artisan's Head

Were you to woo an Artisan and present the object of your passion with gifts of gold and gems, the Artisan would no doubt be flattered. But if you quietly planted a rosebush in the yard, repaired the falling-down shed out back, cooked a meal, or even baked a loaf of bread, you'd be far more likely to win an Artisan's heart.

Not all Artisans have been disappointed by empty promises. But that is how many of them have come to align themselves with things that are bigger than human conceit. Artisans distrust the man-made world; they reject consumerism, commercialism, and the cult of the new. You won't find an Artisan holding court

All that is gold does not glitter; not all those that wander are lost. —J.R.R. TOLKIEN

Casual

Spiritual

at a trendy café, nibbling foie gras after a day of doing damage with the gold card; Artisans seek far more ancient and vastly more reliable ways of being.

At the root of the Artisan's character is a yearning for what is real. This yearning is evident in all aspects of the Artisan's life, from a belief in natural healing (as opposed to high-tech medicine) to a penchant for 100 percent cotton clothing (instead of easy-care synthetics) to a preference for country living (over city life). The less processed a thing is, the more the Artisan is apt to like it—or at least not be suspicious of it.

The Artisan's pursuit of the real could be the result of any number of circumstances. An insecure upbringing in which things were not as they seemed, or a particularly traumatic childhood separation could prompt a person to reject the slick, packaged version of the American Dream. Likewise, an overprivileged upbringing, in which the rough edges of reality were smoothed at each turn, may have instilled in the Artisan a desire to experience the world at its most raw. Of course, there are also softer circumstances from which Artisans may emerge. Perhaps they were reared in an environment where honesty, thrift, self-sacrifice, and neighborliness were emphasized; or maybe they came from a long line of love, as the song goes.

Whatever their early influences might have been, adult Artisans are rarely pretentious, flashy, or dramatic. On the contrary, most are low-key and laid-back; they seek to lead a life of integrity and simplicity.

Familial Bliss

Most Artisans are extremely giving and will readily reach out to those who are in trouble. But their behavior is not just altruistic: it fulfills in them a deep need to belong. Artisans are, in a word, tribal. They are happiest and feel most grounded when they have a clearly defined role within a larger group, and they ensure their place of honor by making themselves useful or, more likely, indispensable.

If a natural family doesn't grow around an Artisan, he or she will subconsciously collect or embrace a familylike unit. Within this tribe, the Artisan comforts the distraught, tends the sick, and coaches the shy. The role the Artisan plays is heroic, but it's a quiet sort of heroism that happens so slowly and with so few fireworks that the Artisan's role could easily go unnoticed.

Nurturing

The Rhythms of Life

A fresh armload of flowers and the purring of an old cat, the hum of cicadas and the smell of rich compost, the mud after rain and the glittering branches of icy trees after sleet—everything in nature is beautiful to the Artisan.

But there is more to nature's appeal than beauty: many an Artisan's mental health depends on the out-of-doors.

Because they tend to be quiet, Artisans can seem as calm and serene as an unrippled pond on a lazy summer day. Beneath the surface, however, they teem with emotion. Prone to inner turmoil, Artisans are always trying to find a place of peace where they can be free from conflict and confusion. Though the search is mostly metaphorical, Artisans really do find serenity when they give themselves over to nature.

Hiking, camping, swimming, sailing, bicycling, skiing,

rock climbing, shooting the rapids—nearly every outdoor activity is compelling to Artisans. But they are perhaps happiest when they are actively working the land. And that means gardening.

Artisans look forward to the rituals of the seasons, and in any given household, they are most likely the ones who rake the leaves, plant the bulbs, and prune the shrubs year after year. Gardening does wonders for the Artisan's mind and spirit, not only because the activity is both meditative and useful, but also because Mother Nature makes the schedule and each task—

You can't get spoiled if you do your own ironing. —MERYL STREEP

planting, cultivating, harvesting—has a season by which Artisans can set their internal clocks. The Artisans' deep sense of time is determined by crocuses, first snows, migrating geese, and the length of the days.

To Be Is to Do

Perhaps the most telling aspect of the Artisan character is this: Artisans show love by doing. The friend who makes a gift of a dried-herb wreath from her garden is probably an Artisan, as is the neighbor who bakes a cake for your birthday, the aunt who knits you an afghan, and the mate who polishes all your shoes while you're sleeping. To the Artisan, a gift of loving labor is far more valuable than any gold watch purchased at a jewelry store.

Acts of love are the Artisans' currency, and they give them freely. When it comes to actual cash, however, Artisans would rather save it than spend it. This doesn't mean they're cheap; rather, it reflects a set of morals. Many Artisans believe that thrift is a virtue; many more believe that wastefulness is a sin.

Some Artisans are acutely aware of the glut of "stuff" in the world—particularly useless, badly made stuff—and don't necessarily want to buy into a cycle of consumerism. Then there are those who want their money to do some good. These Artisans will not invest in companies that pay low wages to Third World workers, overpackage their products, or harm animals or the environment.

In every aspect of their lives, Artisans strive to tread gently on the earth; this means they'll recycle or reuse everything they can. A hard-core Artisan

You May Be an Artisan If . . .

- You're more likely to use an old Mixmaster than a new Cuisinart.
- You enjoy virtually any activity that requires you to wear shorts.
- You'd rather have a pond than a swimming pool.
- Pets are allowed, even encouraged, on your bed.
- No matter where you serve your guests, they seem to like your kitchen best.
- You brake for yard sales.
- You'd rather register at the Home Depot than at Tiffany's.
- When a stray animal is found in your neighborhood, you're the first one to be called.
- You learned needlepoint, crocheting, knitting, and/or tatting from your grandmother.
- You know what a dibble is used for.
- Your favorite time of day is before anyone else has gotten up.

- You have more than three cats.
- You belong to the local food co-op.
- You actually use your canvas shopping bags.
- You fell in love with your house because it had a mudroom.
- You recycled before recycling was the law.
- You'd rather keep a beehive than wear one.
- Your other car's a bicycle.
- For aches and pains, you prefer herbal tea to aspirin.
- You can use the word "ylang-ylang" in a sentence.
- For every bed in your house you have at least one down comforter.
- The first thing you do when you walk into a hotel room is open all the shades.
- You get more excited about an invitation to a picnic than a black-tie event.
- You suspect that handwritten recipes taste better than recipes from cookbooks.
- You're dismayed by the high cost of living, but you gladly pay extra for hand-milled soap, free-range chickens, and beeswax candles.
- You know your rising sign.
- Your idea of makeup is Chap Stick.
- You've witnessed the birth of a colt.
- You're a card-carrying member of PETA.

would never buy a new car if the old jalopy was running just fine. Likewise, he or she would rather resole a favorite pair of shoes than buy new ones. But when Artisans really do need something new, they'll buy the very best that they can afford. After all, they want it to last.

All for Love

Though many Artisans are romantic and very sexual, what they ultimately seek in a love relationship is a working partnership. They find true joy in the day-to-day domestic pleasures that a stable home life affords. Simple activities, like eating a home-cooked meal out-of-doors or going to bed early and snuggling into a wind-dried comforter, are far more precious to the Artisan than splashy nights on the town.

In love, Artisans tend to dedicate themselves wholeheartedly to the happiness of their partner. They take on a tremendous amount of responsibility within a relationship and fiercely protect their loved ones from the slings and arrows of the cold, cruel world. Whether they know it or not, Artisans give what they themselves hope to get. They want to be adored and cared for in the same way they care for and adore others, and with the same intensity. Artisans thrive in such matches; with their love by their side they are able to weather storms and survive catastrophes with awesome strength and steadfastness.

Unfortunately, not all Artisan partnerships can achieve or sustain such a smooth give-and-take. Artisans can have a very difficult time asking for what they want; their most honest language is a language of doing, not saying. So it takes a perceptive partner to know that Artisans, in spite of their self-effacing manner, need lots of attention, encouragement, affection, and support. If Artisans

suspect that their labors of love are being taken for granted, they might, in desperation, resort to guilt trips, tantrums (silent or otherwise), and even acts of vengeance.

Artisans are prone to jealousy, and their green-eyed monster is surprisingly fierce. Having made great sacrifices in the name of love, the Artisan cannot bear to be rejected or even temporarily ignored in favor of a cuter, cleverer, or sexier candidate. Anyone who has ever loved an Artisan knows very well that hell has no wrath like an Artisan scorned.

HOW TO TURN ANY ROOM INTO AN ARTISAN ROOM

Some Artisans live to decorate and have a great flair for creating inviting spaces, no matter what their budget happens to be. Others are less inclined to bother, but by taking these ten simple and not-so-simple steps, anyone can turn a mere room into an airy, soulful Artisan space.

1. Paint the ceiling and the trim white; use a flat finish for the ceiling and a semigloss finish for the trim. Paint the walls linen white with an eggshell finish.

2. Remove heavy rugs and wall-to-wall carpeting. If there are wood floors underneath, have them stripped to the palest possible shade. For maximum sun reflection, coat them with high-gloss polyurethane.

3. If the floors can't be stripped, paint them with a pale gray deck paint.

4. Cover all linoleum with sisal rugs or flooring.

5. Replace drapes or blinds with lighter-than-air window coverings, or leave the windows uncurtained. If privacy is an issue, try layers of lace or pull-down shades in cutwork patterns.

6. If your ceilings are low, hand-paint wide vertical stripes on the walls in a shade slightly darker than linen white. This will create an illusion of height.

7. Create a seating area by the dominant window of the room. Use two mismatched high-backed wooden chairs and a round glass-topped or wicker table on top of a braided rug.

8. A living room or family room should include a deep, comfy sofa in a neutral color; at least one armchair draped with vintage fabric, a favorite quilt, or a shawl; and a wooden coffee table in any size or shape.

9. Accessorize with antique floor lamps, small table lamps, and pillows. Make liberal use of plants, baskets, pottery, and scatter rugs.

10. Take paintings and prints off their hooks and lean them against the walls.

It's a Keeper

Though Artisans are famously nonmaterialistic, in the sense that they don't care about the monetary worth of things, they do tend to forge strong sentimental attachments to objects and can end up with an enormous number of possessions, including a basement full of "future projects." This kind of hoarding could drive tidier types a little crazy. But where others see junk or clutter, the Artisan sees orphans and ugly ducklings that just need a little love—but that's only one reason why it's so difficult for Artisans to throw anything away.

To understand the psychological basis of the Artisan's hoarding instincts, picture a house with an attic, a main floor, and a basement. The attic represents the past. It is filled with historical artifacts (Grandpa's immigration papers, Aunt Lucille's wedding dress), childhood mementos (report cards, finger paintings), and objects that have been outgrown (macramé owls, rock posters).

The basement is where unborn projects live. It represents the future. Chairs without upholstery, cups without saucers, saucers without cups—these will eventually be repaired and refurbished, and placed into service on the main floor.

The main floor is a living, breathing present where flowers are arranged, salads are tossed, phones are answered. Most important, it is where the Artisan finds his or her place between the past and the future.

Artisans need to know that they belong somewhere. Home provides tangible evidence of their past and an assurance that they will still be needed in the future; it provides them with proof of a personal history.

Inside the Artisan's Home

A happy home is of supreme importance to the Artisan. He or she will take great care to ensure harmony and to make everyone—both insiders and outsiders—feel comfortable and welcome. There is a strong sense of hearth in the Artisan's

dwelling; it is a place for warm gatherings where grandmas, babies, scruffy neighbor kids, dogs, and any number of friends and strangers can come together for a holiday meal or a backyard barbecue. It doesn't matter if none of the plates match or if half of the guests sit on folding chairs; joy is the goal, and the Artisan promotes it in every way.

In the Artisan home, "casual" is the operative word. Don't look for precious *objets* all gilded and glittering, and don't expect to see sleek modern pieces that

honor engineering. What Artisans seek is soul. Let others buy new products that have been designed for mass consumption; Artisans want things that have been handcrafted with love by actual individuals. From painted window boxes to cross-stitched pillowcases, the Artisan responds to pieces that are imperfect or so worn with age and use that they seem to have grown out of the earth itself.

Gifts of Nature

If you were to ask an Artisan what most mattered in home design, it is doubtful that he or she could name styles or kinds of furnishings. This is because Artisans, first and foremost, crave earth, air, fire, and water. Give them land, a spacious deck or a mossy greenhouse, a pond with a couple of ducks, a lofty barn with dust-specked sunlight—these gifts of nature will excite and sustain them.

Even in urban settings, Artisans seek to re-create the feeling of nature. They'll keep their windows bare in order to maximize sunlight, and they will most likely nurture a small forest of houseplants. The tiniest of patios will be cherished by the Artisan, filled with plants or strung with a hammock. Airy, organic materials such as wicker, sisal, and cotton appeal to Artisans; they'd rather not weigh themselves down with heavy furnishings or forbiddingly formal rooms.

Equally important to Artisans is relaxation. They like cozy corners, deliciously deep chairs, beds piled high with pillows, and lived-in rooms that ooze comfort. Given a choice between living in a grand gilded palace and holing up in a comfy old fishing lodge, the Artisan will invariably choose the lodge. Artisans need to kick their shoes off, drape themselves on furniture or floors, and let their bodies be as their bodies will be.

Artisans are do-it-yourselfers who want to get their hands dirty and don't mind breaking a sweat. An Artisan who can't actually build a

home from scratch may tackle such tasks as stripping woodwork, hand-stenciling walls, or clearing land. If the job requires hours of grueling labor, so be it: few things please Artisans as much as completing an ambitious, worthy project with their own hands.

It follows that Artisans cherish old and even neglected structures. When house hunting, Artisans don't bother to look at new homes in planned developments; they seek out decrepit houses on vast plots of land. An Artisan can turn a falling-down chicken coop into a charming cottage, or an old garage into a sweet, snug guesthouse.

The Artisan Touch

The range of Artisan interiors is vast. At the minimalist end of the spectrum are those Artisans who value the lean aesthetic of the Shaker and Mission styles and find beauty in the character of unembellished wood and the integrity of simple design.

At the other end of the spectrum are those Artisans who gather stuff around them as if their very possessions were a baffle against the outside world. Such Artisans compose rooms that are complex visual feasts, where photos of family and friends coexist with cushy chairs, dried flowers, teapots, candlesticks, and vintage fabrics draped on tables. What the two styles have in common is natural materials, a patina of age, and, perhaps most important, an emphasis on texture.

Texture is a key element in every Artisan interior. Artisans will tear down a ceiling in order to expose ancient beams, and will take a sledgehammer to Sheetrock-clad walls to liberate hand-hewn bricks. Crumbling plaster walls excite Artisans, as do barn-board floors; these honest, homey elements speak of authenticity and make Artisans feel connected with the history of their homes.

The Artisan Alphabet

Adirondack chairs • afghans • animals • armoires • Arts and Crafts • attics • baby buggies • Ball jars • barn boards • barns • basketry • bay windows • beaches • benches • birdhouses • braided rugs • bricks • bungalows • candles • canoes • carriage houses • children's art • Christmas • claw-footed tubs • colored glass • cottages • cotton • cross-stitching • denim • dinghies • distressed paint • docks • dried flowers • Easter • exposed beams • florist's buckets • folk art • gardens • grandfather clocks • greenhouses • hammocks • hand-loomed rugs • hankies • hemp • herbs • Hoosier cabinets • hutches • indigenous plants • ivy-colored walls • kindred spirits • lanterns • lighthouses • manual typewriters • Mission furniture • moss • mudrooms • muslin • naive art • oak • old lace • outdoor showers • pansies • paper • patina • picket fences • picnic baskets • ponds • porches • potpourri • pottery • produce • quilts • raffia • rag dolls • rambling rosebushes • rattan • recycling • river rocks • rocking chairs • scrapbooks • screen doors • seed packets • Shaker furniture • sisal • snow-shoes • steamer trunks • stenciled designs • stone fireplaces • stone walls • tea cozies • teapots • terra-cotta • texture • twine • unbleached linen • vegetable dyes • weathervanes • wildflowers • wind chimes • windows • wreaths • yoga • the Zodiac

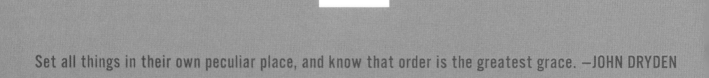

Set all things in their own peculiar place, and know that order is the greatest grace. —JOHN DRYDEN

Idealist

IF THE IDEALIST were to have a literary theme, it might be "humankind against human nature." Like every person on this earth, the Idealist is subject to the daily struggles of relationships, family, and day-to-day survival. The Idealist approach, however, is not to absorb or integrate these messy realities but to

Principled

conquer them. Idealists want definite solutions to problems and will invest significant time, money, and energy to achieve uncompromised results.

In their own way, Idealists are warriors. And they do not go haphazardly into battle. With strategy, foresight, and good sense on their side, they fight for what they love, need, and long for.

While they may have a rich and intense emotional life, Idealists find their strength among what is tangible. In order to feel truly successful they need

Logical

proof—real physical evidence—of progress and a promising future: an orderly home, an established career, a healthy body, a solid financial portfolio. Idealists build strong foundations and stand firm in the concrete world.

Inside the Idealist's Head

Idealists are great planners. When a vacation is scheduled, the Idealist will start collecting literature months in advance, researching the pros and cons of various destinations, activities, and attractions. By the time the trip begins, he or she will have mapped out a budgeted itinerary that would be the envy of any military commander.

On a larger scale, many Idealists plot and follow a master life plan. They usually begin organizing their lives at a young age: Idealists are the ones who know which high school courses will benefit them in graduate school. They want the right degree from the right college, the best entry-level job, and the position with the most potential for advancement. They're apt to start saving for retirement while still in their twenties, and they'll gladly do all the research required in order to make smart long-term investments. They're the ones who coined the phrase "ten-year plan."

Competitive

Inquisitive

DISCIPLINED

Less is more. —LUDWIG MIES VAN DER ROHE (quoting Robert Browning)

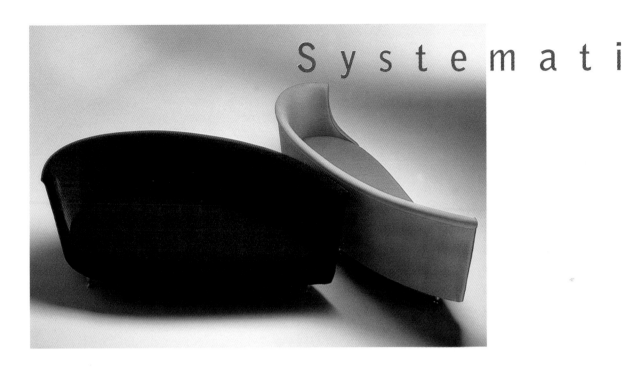

Systematic

The motivating factor behind such dedicated plotting and planning is this: Idealists place their faith in systems. Visionaries may be guided by their inner, "sacred" selves; Artisans may find their strength within circles of love; Adventurers may rely on destiny to deliver them. But Idealists do not trust the unreliable ebb and flow of emotion, spirituality, inspiration, or chance. Instead, they construct fortresses outside themselves. They utilize tried-and-true methods; they solicit expert advice, check track records, and do the math. In short, Idealists set clear goals and strive for success by doing things the "right" way.

Erasing the Past

Some Idealists forged their methodical habits early in life by following in the footsteps of strong, clearly directed parents.

Unfortunately, however, other Idealists were reared in households marred by poverty, ignorance, or abuse. Such Idealists likely became independent at an early age. Some may have been forced to take on adult responsibilities in childhood; others may have experienced early life as a time of insecurity, never knowing what the next day would bring. There are many Idealists who spent precious childhood hours plotting a life of success far removed from their roots. Still others simply decided, at some point in their young lives, to really make something of themselves.

In any case, few adult Idealists embrace the past. In fact, many seek to erase it. It's quite common to find Idealist interiors in which there is not one clue to the occupant's personal history—no mementos, no photographs, no heirlooms, no hand-me-downs. Some Idealist homes are so thoroughly scoured of personal touches they could pass as Witness Protection Program houses. But Idealists, especially those breakaway kids who escaped unfortunate beginnings, are

not interested in remembering their past; they are in the business of re-creating themselves. In fact, the archetypal Idealist home, with its smooth, uncluttered surfaces and its distinct lack of personal touches is, symbolically, a blank slate.

The Beauty of Systems

Why do Idealists love systems? Because they can be counted on. While the passion plays of life simmer and explode all around them, Idealists know that systems quietly tick along, doing their prosaic but essential jobs. The heating, the plumbing, the electricity, the car engine—these sound, reliable systems allow life to run smoothly.

Idealists believe that systems have to be established and maintained in order for any human progress to take place. And so they focus on frameworks. By nature, Idealists are architects, not interior designers; they're the ones who

You May Be an Idealist If . . .

- Your CDs are arranged in alphabetical order.
- Your other car is a cigarette boat.
- You know how to program your VCR.
- You know the difference between an Eames and a Bertoia.
- The lights in your home are on dimmers, timers, or motion detectors.
- You often give Omaha steaks or Fruit-of-the-Month club memberships as presents.
- Your wristwatch also functions as an alarm clock, a barometer, a stopwatch, and a night-light.
- You've taken a Club Med vacation.
- When cooking for yourself, you judge your success on how few plates and utensils you've used.
- You consider E-mail a godsend.
- You know your cholesterol count.
- You put your spare change into an automatic coin sorter.
- You always back up your hard drive.
- Your Christmas would be much merrier if Santa came down the chimney and took stuff away.
- You trade your old skiing equipment for new skiing equipment at the end of each winter.
- You lease a new car every year.
- Even though you've never had a weight problem, you drink diet soda and buy low-fat foods.
- You get rid of newspapers and magazines immediately after you've read them.
- You have specific nights of the week on which you do laundry, go grocery shopping, and work out at the gym.

- You keep to a household budget.
- Your coffeemaker and your alarm clock are synchronized.
- You can use the word "conundrum" in a sentence.
- As a child, you loved Erector sets and Lego blocks.
- All your maps are folded correctly.
- You own a cell phone, a beeper, a good pair of binoculars, a sophisticated home security system, a digital camera, a video camera, a laser disc player, and a pair of night-vision goggles.
- Your favorite color is "goes with everything."
- You wouldn't buy a dog unless you were sure it would guard the house.
- The words "impulse buy" are not in your vocabulary.
- You're ready for an IRS audit at any time—in fact, you keep an "In Case I Get Audited" file.

Good order is the foundation of all good things. —EDMUND BURKE

make sure that foundations are dug properly and that buildings are true and hale. They think ahead to the future and make decisions based on the long haul, suppressing their momentary impulses and making logical choices based on solid information. While others tend to the soul, the heart, and the imagination, Idealists make sure that the buildings that house these blithe spirits won't fall down. They are the engineers of civilization.

Sometimes the Idealists' belief in systems is expressed in subtle ways. Many of them just plain enjoy machines. The businessman who disappears into the garage every weekend to tinker with a vintage car, and the human resources

manager who can't wait to get home and log on to the Internet are both finding refuge in the clean reality of self-contained systems. Likewise, people who choose careers as scientists, mathematicians, tax consultants, mechanics, computer programmers, or surgeons are placing themselves within systems that have their own indisputable rules. Certainly there is room for creativity within such jobs, but each one has predetermined parameters. And that is where the Idealist likes to dwell: within a solid framework that cannot and will not wiggle and crash, because it is based on laws that are not subject to human speculation or interference.

Answering to the Inner Commander

Though some Idealists insist that they are weak-willed, most are actually highly disciplined. Inside of the Idealist is a commander who demands that they jog three times a week or follow a strict beauty regimen or attend every single Quark class at the adult ed center, even if they don't feel like it. This inner parent is the keeper of the Idealist's to-do list. And only when Idealists have achieved the figurative clean desk at the end of the day are they allowed to watch hours of trashy television, search the Net for perverted Websites, or go out and ski the meanest mountains.

Idealists are not spontaneous folk who'll drop everything whenever an

Jump-Starting Your Inner Idealist

Of the four personality types, the Idealist is least likely to think of shopping as a sport. Since they rarely acquire possessions on a whim or in a fit of passion, Idealists aren't usually limited to decorating around what they already have—which, while liberating, may leave them wondering where to start. Some approaches:

The form-follows-function approach. Ask yourself what has to be accomplished in the space. Make a detailed list, considering such elements as seating (how many visitors are you likely to have at once?); natural light (do you need full shades to block out the morning sun?); artificial light (reading lamps? general lighting? dimmers?); noise levels (if you plan to play opera CDs at full blast in a condo, you'll probably need thick carpeting); and storage. Consider the activities that will go on in a room (watching TV, eating dinner, sleeping, dressing, reading the paper) and figure out the best way to accommodate each one.

Finally, sketch out a floor plan and take measurements. Be sure to note the location of electrical outlets, the height and width of windows, the swing area of each door and the width of the doorways (to make sure that credenza can actually be moved in).

Shopping becomes much easier when you know, for instance, that you need two sofas at right angles that can't be more than x inches long, x inches deep, and x inches high (to avoid blocking the view). These measurements will significantly narrow the field and can be a real confidence-booster when confronted with a bewildering sea of options.

The do-it-for-me approach. Look through home design magazines (shelter mags, as they're known in the trade), and tear out photographs of rooms that appeal to you. Creating a beautiful room can be as simple as going to the hairdresser; since most high-end furniture stores have designers on staff, you can simply arrive with a photograph and say, "Give me this." *Tip:* Bring exact measurements.

The überpiece approach. Determine the single most important piece of furniture in a room—the bed, perhaps, or the dining table or the sofa. Shop for that piece and that piece only. Shop hard. Look high and low until you've found the one that is better than all the rest and makes you shout, "Eureka!" Buy it. Once it's installed in your home, it will set the tone for your interior. And having shopped well for your überpiece, you'll already know where to shop for the rest of your furniture.

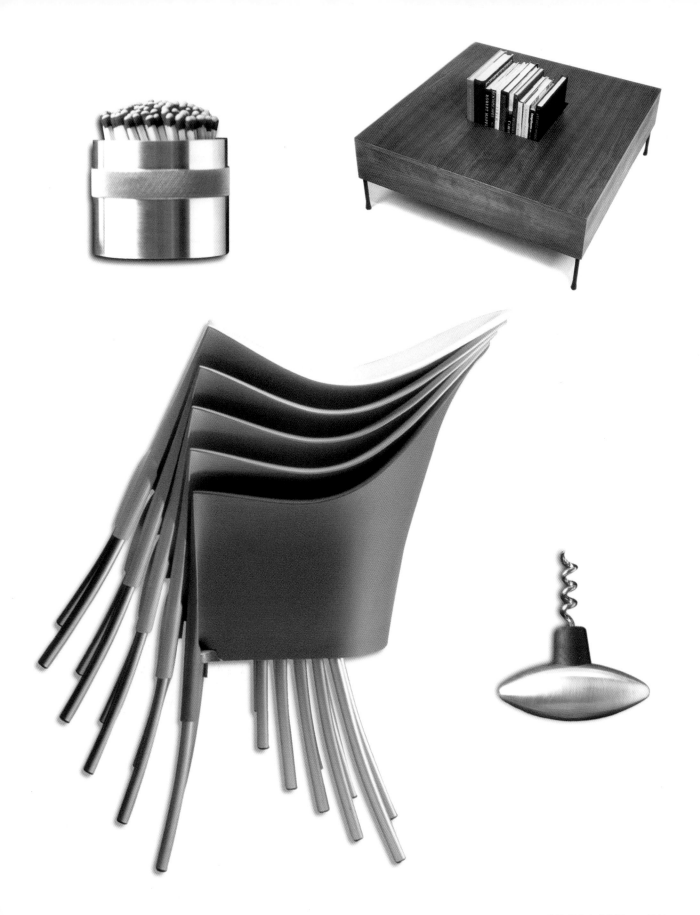

The Quality Question

Go shopping with an Idealist, point to a sofa, and ask, "What do you think?" The Idealist will probably start processing information about cost, size, practicality, and soundness of construction. The Idealist will probably *not* squeal, "It's adorable! Buy it!"

Though everybody gets an illogical urge now and then, the concept of impulsiveness is by and large alien to the Idealist. This is true because Idealists are not usually driven by that vague mode of personal expression known as style. Rather, they want only what they need, but they want what they need to be the best.

Buying the best is important to Idealists. There are two main reasons for this. One is that many Idealists don't trust their own taste. They do not tend to have immediate, powerful responses to nuances of color, shape, and subtext. Instead, they pay attention to concrete concerns: What company manufactures this sofa? Does it have a reputation for quality and service? If this purchase doesn't live up to my expectations, will I be able to return it?

Beauty is subjective; Idealists are objective.

Which explains the Idealist's other reason for wanting to buy only the best: spending more on high-end or status-label products serves as a kind of insurance policy. They can be pretty sure that, besides being reliable, and preferably guaranteed, the product is attractive and appropriate. Once again the Idealist has bought into a reliable system.

Take It All Off

Most Idealists believe that minimalism is a virtue. Their motto? When in doubt, throw it out.

It's not just a dislike of clutter that turns Idealists toward minimalism. Many have a true appreciation of negative space—that is, areas that contain nothing but air. They don't want to disguise the bones of a room, and would rather celebrate design details such as high ceilings or interesting windows than obscure or overwhelm them with mere furnishings.

Many Idealists see rooms as interiorscapes. In a long, low room banked by windows, Idealists will carefully choose furniture that does not interfere with the horizontal vista. Likewise, an Idealist will preserve the integrity of a curved wall by keeping it free of decorative elements.

The Idealist's talent for editing can result in spaces of exquisite simplicity and serenity. Some Idealist interiors resemble Zen gardens; others utilize no-nonsense materials like concrete and aluminum to achieve a stripped-down, industrial aesthetic.

Like Adventurers, Idealists resist arbitrary borders and assigned spaces. They prefer open floor plans that allow them to adapt areas to suit their needs, and won't hesitate to knock down useless walls or even board up badly positioned windows. Whether located in a high-rise penthouse, a suburban contemporary, or a reclaimed loft space, it is an uncompromising eye and disciplined hand that goes into the creation of the archetypal Idealist space.

Excuse Me, Your Passion Is Showing

Some Idealist homes look like art galleries. That's because some Idealist homes *are* art galleries.

Though usually logical and clearheaded, it's very much within the Idealist nature to pursue a hobby and allow it to grow into a magnificent obsession. If an Idealist collects, say, contemporary sculpture, then much of his or her home might be designed to display it. The audiophile Idealist will have an acoustically correct room that houses spectacular equipment and 100,000 CDs. Gourmet Idealists install professional-quality kitchens in their homes, and cyber-Idealists maintain temperature-controlled computer rooms. Idealists often manage to justify such mad expenditures: the kitchen adds resale value to their home, and the CDs will become a valuable collection.

Neatness Counts

Many Idealists like to have a single look carried throughout the home. They are partial to modular furniture that can be reconfigured as the need arises, and they like cool, clean materials such as marble, slate, glass, concrete, leather, chrome, aluminum, and steel.

Idealists take delight in finding invisible solutions to design problems. Most would rather have recessed lighting than lamps, especially because lamps have untidy cords. They favor custom cabinets, particularly if they're disguised as a wall of panels without visible hardware. And electronic controls are an Idealist's dream: they want to push a button and make all the blinds silently open.

Many Idealist design choices come from one simple truth: Idealists can't stand messiness. Whether they live in a cramped basement apartment or a sprawling estate, Idealists want their homes to look neat and tidy at all times. They will not be able to relax in a room until newspapers, toys, spare change, and stray shoes have been picked up and put away—each in its proper place.

The Idealist Alphabet

aluminum • aquariums • architecture • automatism • Bauhaus • black-and-white • blinds • built-in cabinets • carpeting • CD towers • cell phones • chaos theory • chrome • computers • condos • dimmer switches • Eames chairs • electronics • engineering • Erector sets • ergonomic design • exercise equipment • flagstone • food processors • Futurism • gadgets • garbage disposals • gas fireplaces • geometry • glass • glass bricks • good knives • granite • graphics • gravel • gyms • heat lamps • hedges • high-tech design • home theater systems • indoor swimming pools • industrial materials • information • intercoms • investments • Jacuzzis • king-size beds • leather • lofts • machines • metal • minimalism • Modernism • modular furniture • Mondrian • monochromatic color schemes • Murphy beds • new stuff • organization • Peg-Board • photography • pin spots • planes • platform beds • professional-quality kitchen equipment • QWERTY • Ayn Rand • security systems • shoji screens • showers • skylights • skyscrapers • slate • sliding glass doors • spas • speakerphones • spiral staircases • stacking chairs • steel • stone • storage systems • surround sound • tiled surfaces • tongue-and-groove joints • tools • track lighting • Universal Design • videophones • virtual reality • white space • Frank Lloyd Wright • yachts • Zen

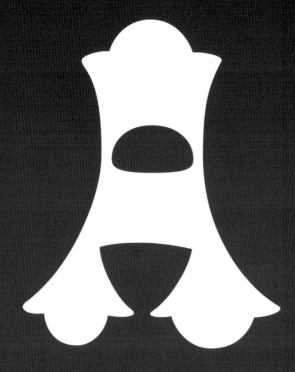

The mark of genius is an incessant activity of mind. Genius is a spiritual greed. —V. S. PRITCHETT

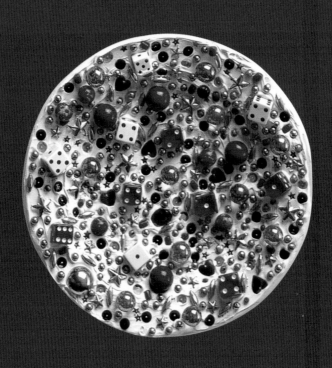

Artistic

ADVENTURERS LIVE in an almost constant state of yearning. "Anything but boredom" could be their mantra; they thrive on sensory pleasures, intellectual challenges, human contact, sport, and spiritual pursuits. Like Visionaries, Adventurers require beauty in their lives, but they never want their possessions to slow them down: Adventurers want action, and they want it now.

Auntie Mame said, "Life is a banquet and most poor suckers are starving to death." Adventurers agree. They want to experience all that life

Flamboyant

has to offer, especially those bits that are profound, rich, outrageous, funny, and unusual. The archetypal Adventurer thinks of his or her life as a work in progress, with each new phase—whether it be a new style, home, career, or relationship—providing an opportunity for personal evolution . . . or at least fun.

Adventurers dread missing out on anything; no parade is allowed to pass them by. Borrowing from a huge range of cultures and disciplines, making up rules as they go along, and living in the bright moment, Adventurers are agents of change, and they are not interested in a life without risk.

Inside the Adventurer's Head

Some people see life as a series of problems to be solved. Not Adventurers. They're on this earth to mix things up, to throw stuff in the air and see where it lands. They believe in unlimited possibilities and infinite variety, and they thumb their noses at what is conventional, safe, predictable, or, God forbid, respectable. Breaking through boundaries and bending the rules is their joy; predictability is their poison.

There is a circuslike quality to the Adventurer lifestyle. Dramatic action happens simultaneously in at least three rings. With balancing acts, displays of bravado, dramatic feats, and a bit of clowning, the Adventurer plays the roles of acrobat, aerialist, lion tamer, and ringmaster. All this activity is evidence of an agile intellect that makes connections between seemingly disparate things.

The Adventurer mind leaps beyond categories and definitions, seeking out

Playful

Inventive

DRAMATIC

"In the U.S. you have to be a deviant or die of boredom."

—WILLIAM BURROUGHS

common threads between cultures, eras, and disciplines. Socially, they tend to be genuinely blind to strata of class, wealth, or education. Instead, they pay attention to originality and high spirits, and they delight in the variety of a life that may include fencing lessons, jam sessions, trips to remote Latin American villages, amateur rocketry, and freelance mural-painting. It is juicy diversity that enriches the Adventurer's heart and soul.

The Voice of Lawlessness

Adventurers run on passion. It is their fuel, their fire, their reason for being. Volatile and demonstrative, Adventurers do not logically map out a path through life; they follow visceral responses and gut reactions.

Most Adventurers believe that rules do not apply to them. Though they may or may not actually live outside the law, they do not trust systems or tried-and-true methods. One would be hard-pressed to find an instruction manual, rule book, or self-help book in the Adventurer's home—though one might spot a Ouija board, a deck of tarot cards, or the *I-ching*. Adventurers seek connection with a universe of ideas and emotions that cannot be contained by cultural boundaries or traditional ways of being.

To Adventurers, faintness of heart is the only true failure. They tend to burn the candle at both ends, throwing themselves passionately into activities, projects, and relationships. Their behavior can be extreme, but there is an underlying reason for their urgency: At their very core, Adventurers are acutely aware of their own mortality. They leapfrog over conventional ways of doing things because they sense the brackets around their own lives. They want to experience all they can before their time is up. They also want to make a mark on the world.

Adventurers resist conformity. They can have a terrible time accomplishing basic things, like earning a living, because they do not want to subscribe to established sets of rules. They fear that, by choosing a conventional career and buying into an expected code of behavior, they might lose sight of their larger purpose—that is, whatever unique contribution they are destined to make to society. The dilemma: getting a job might keep them from their work.

Some Adventurers never manage to build a bridge between their desire for greatness and their need simply to survive. Instead, they keep on moving, and they look at each phase of their development as part of a life well lived. Words like "inconsistent" and "immature" may sometimes be pinned on the Adventurer, but so might words like "extraordinary" and "original."

- You can converse in Cantonese, land a 40-pound bluefish, and play six musical instruments, but can't balance your checkbook.
- You have no idea what half the keys on your key ring are for.
- You don't dread large parties—only small and intimate ones.
- You've never changed a battery "just in case." You wait until the flashlight no longer works or the boom box conks out.
- You have, at some point in your life, either hitch-hiked or picked up a hitchhiker.
- Your car engine has seized up because you forgot to check the oil.
- None of your maps are folded right.
- You have your hair cut whenever the mood strikes, instead of making regular appointments.
- You'd rather wear fabulous fake jewelry than con-servative real jewelry.
- You could live on appetizers and desserts.
- You own a fez.
- The backseat of your car is an auxiliary closet.
- You believe that half the fun of traveling is having conversations with strangers.
- You never put name tags on your possessions, even when you went to summer camp.
- You'd rather wear a beehive than keep one.
- At some point in your life, you've tied a maraschino cherry stem with your tongue, eaten the worm from a tequila bottle, or won a limbo contest.

- You practice creative multitasking—playing the harmonica while you drive, perhaps, or washing your underwear while you shower.
- Your car routinely runs out of gas.
- Your freezer routinely runs out of ice.
- You pack two suitcases for a weekend trip but forget your toothbrush.
- Your friends tell you that events start earlier than they actually do so there's a chance you'll be on time.

Mañana

Adventurers expend energy in great bursts. Many actually enjoy performing in pressure-cooker situations and believe they're at their blazing best when pressed and stressed. This may explain why some Adventurers procrastinate. It is very much in character for an Adventurer to pick up a brush and repaint the entire bathroom the night before a party. After such bouts of overextension, the Adventurer's downtime can become a festival of lethargy in which all activity, including basic tasks like combing one's hair, comes to a complete stop.

At home, Adventurers excel at interesting, ambitious jobs such as trimming the hedges into imaginative shapes, decorating the Christmas tree, and shopping. They're far less useful when it comes to vacuuming, dusting, and washing the dishes. Routine maintenance is not only supremely boring to the Adventurer, it also seems futile. After all, the very same jobs will have to be performed over and over again, and that kind of monotony can make an Adventurer roll over and play dead. Adventurers' burning belief that every moment is precious can make them resent tasks that robots could perform.

Adventurers in Love

Ah, love! The Adventurer is smitten. Birds sing, bells ring, and the Adventurer bestows gestures of affection on his or her glowing beloved. Will it last?

Adventurers are devilishly charming, but they require a tremendous amount of patience, understanding, and attention. What Adventurers often need in a long-term relationship is a rudder, someone to keep them steady while the waves crash, the tides go in and out, and—scariest of all—the seas grow calm. People who love Adventurers sometimes find themselves in the shadows, expected to play a role that resembles more an indulgent parent than a lover.

Adventurers, for their part, tend to be terrified of long-term commitments because they need to feel that love is constantly being renewed. They can't tolerate a clingy, needy partner, nor can they abide a mate who imposes inflexible rules and regulations. They want their loved one to grow along with them and always be open to change and surprise.

Inside the Adventurer's Home

Adventurers' homes are filled with people, music, books, and things to pick up, touch, and play with. Of all the personality types, Adventurers need the most living space, if only to accommodate their many interests. They could make good use of a ballroom, a billiard room, a spa, a chapel, a radio tower, a lounge, twelve bedrooms, and twenty walk-in closets.

Yet even in a tiny apartment, the Adventurer will manage to create space that's eclectic and amusing. Fun lives at the Adventurer's house; anything can happen there. It is where whims are indulged, dancing is allowed, and shirts and shoes are optional. Adventurers throw their doors open to the world and invite excitement to cross the threshold.

In spirit, if not in style, the Adventurer's home life harks back to the days of the grand salons, when artists, thinkers, and celebrated wits would gather to exchange ideas and make mischief. It is not stillness or sanctuary that the Adventurer asks of home: it is stimulation.

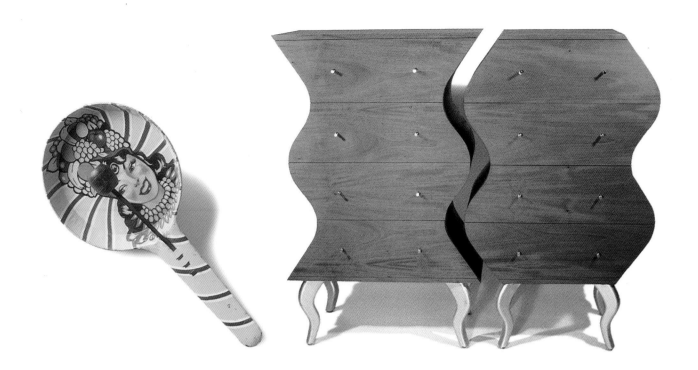

Less is a bore. —ROBERT VENTURI

Don't Fence Me In

Adventurers tend to avoid tiny rooms with doors that close. In fact, they're famous for tearing down walls and for creating windows and half-walls between previously isolated spaces. This is an outward manifestation of a general dislike of boundaries, which in some Adventurers is so pronounced that they suffer from claustrophobia.

Adventurers want an openness between rooms that allows for communication and connection. Even when they are alone, Adventurers like to roam about the house—watering a plant there, noodling a tune on the piano, playing a round of solitaire on the computer—all while talking on

the portable phone. It isn't unusual to find Adventurers' homes in which the distinctions between major living spaces are signaled by little more than the color of the walls or a sudden grouping of furniture.

Adventurers can be happy in almost any place that affords flexibility and elbow room. But perhaps their favorite living space is the loft—and the bigger and emptier the loft, the more the Adventurer likes it. The liberating prospect of high ceilings, oodles of square footage, big windows, and no walls sets the Adventurer's imagination on fire. He or she is free to hang swings from the ceiling; re-create an Italian palazzo, complete with a fully operational fountain; build walls on casters, to be repositioned at will; suspend stained-glass windows on pulleys; or just leave the space raw.

Systematic Idealists and symmetry-loving Visionaries could go mad in such spaces, but Adventurers relish the unexpected.

Color Me Adventurous

Adventurers are creatures of action. They seek out pulse, vibrations, and the chemistry that happens when disparate elements are thrown together. You can see this in their style of entertaining, yet it is perhaps most obvious in their use of color: they have a very strong attraction to complementary color schemes— colors that lie opposite one another on the color wheel. Adventurers respond to the visual twang that occurs when ultramarine is matched with nectarine, when vermilion goes up against viridian, and when lilac is paired with chartreuse. Adventurers would far rather err on the side of garish than be stuck in a quiet-toned home with gentle gradations and whispering neutrals. Hushed color schemes may be soothing to others, but Adventurers will likely be reminded of waiting rooms, funeral parlors, corporations, or other soul-squelching places where Adventurers feel themselves to be alien.

The purest and most thoughtful minds are those which love color the most.—JOHN RUSKIN

The Call of the Wild

The Adventurers' craving for stimulation sends them on a constant search for that which is new, bold, mysterious, or innovative. This nonstop shopping,

however, does not reflect a materialistic turn of mind. Adventurers listen carefully to their own impulses, especially in matters of decor, because they want to stay one step ahead of themselves. Surroundings that are dated or played out can depress them. Adventurers crave those moments when they spot a shocking object, or see a mind-bending museum exhibit, and can šay to themselves, "This changes everything." It is at such times that Adventurers may be inspired to over-haul their style. Such changes are not only cosmetic: to Adventurers they represent nothing less than a leap of personal evolution.

In their quest to make rooms that sparkle with personality, Adventurers may borrow motifs from almost any time or place. But they are rarely purists. Adventurers will go right ahead and mount that African mask on the wall, even if it's plastic and made in Taiwan, or top a $75 Salvation Army sofa with a pillow that cost $150. Consistency and status mean nothing to Adventurers. Home is theater, and nothing is permanent; the sets will come down as easily as they went up.

My Place or Mine?

Adventurers love company. Just as an idea can provoke a full-on redecoration, a new friend or group of friends can throw the Adventurer into raptures of possibilities. And new friends are not uncommon in the Adventurer's world: an Adventurer can set off for the beach in the morning with a familiar pal and end up at dinner that night with five new friends, made that day.

Adventurers keep their homes ready for such spontaneous gatherings. "Ready," in the Adventurer's lexicon, doesn't necessarily mean pristine and polished. It simply means presentable and stocked with provisions. Standard equipment includes an arsenal of games, good food, a well-stocked bar, music, and a large circular table around which meals can be eaten and all-night poker games furiously played.

Most important is the spirit of the Adventurer home: nothing there is too precious to be enjoyed. If, in the course of an evening, a vase is broken or a tray of hors d'oeuvres goes belly up, it's a small price to pay for camaraderie, chemistry, and good cheer.

The Adventurer Alphabet

accordions • Airstream trailers • amateur art • animal-print fabrics • anthropology • artifacts • artifice • AstroTurf • Barbie's Dream House • beach balls • beading • beanbag chairs • birthday cakes • board games • boomerang Formica • bowling balls • bulletin boards • bunk beds • cabanas • casinos • casters • cha-cha records • checkerboards • chopsticks • circles • classic modern design • cocktail lounges • cocktail shakers • cocktail tables • color • confetti • dinettes • elephant-foot umbrella stands • fountains • Graceland • Halloween • harlequin patterns • hat racks • hi-fis • ice buckets • junque • kidney-shaped swimming pools • Kit-cat clocks • kitsch • Las Vegas • lava lamps • lawn ornaments • linoleum • lounge music • Lurex • marbles • Mardi Gras • martini glasses • masks • metaphors • Mexican art • Moderne • mosaics • mounted antlers • movable screens • multiculturalism • Naugahyde • novelty stemware • nylon • open shelving • patios • pendant lamps • plastic • plush • polka dots • princess-style phones • religious statuary • rubber-band balls • rumpus rooms • secondary colors • sequins • split levels • surprise parties • swizzle sticks • theme rooms • tiaras • Trader Vic's • tribal art • trophies • umbrella tables • Velvis (Elvis on velvet) • wild parties • zebra-print fabric

IDEALIST

Visionary

Artisan

ADVENTURER

Intuitive Rooms

The Living Room

OUR GRANDMOTHERS HAD parlors and sitting rooms. We of the thoroughly modern home have living rooms to call our own. The living room can be a sunny place with wraparound windows and rattan furniture, a cushy sunken area with low-slung sofas, or a formal showplace where, in spite of its name, nobody really lives.

The living room is usually the largest room in the house and the first room that visitors see. It tends to set the general design tone for the whole place, which may be why people spend significant time and money decorating it; if one room is going to be perfect, it will be the living room. It represents our public self and puts our tastes on display. It keeps us on our best behavior and makes everyone's posture just a little bit better. Above all others, it is the room that's all dressed up and ready for company.

MATCH THE LIVING ROOM WITH THE TYPE

1. No drapes on windows
2. Off-limits to children and dogs
3. Furniture rearranged one hour ago
4. Twin black leather sofas

A. **The Idealist**
B. **The Adventurer**
C. **The Visionary**
D. **The Artisan**

Answers: The Artisan is most likely to have naked windows; the Visionary would rather keep certain rooms for special occasions; the Adventurer often rearranges furniture; and the Idealist is most likely to have black leather sofas.

The Visionary Living Room

What does the Visionary really want? A fireplace in the living room. And a beautiful work of art to hang over it. And antique andirons. And an Oriental rug. A good one. And an assortment of seating ranging from an antique horsehair sofa to an Empire chair. Gilt-framed mirrors. A tapestry or two. Richly embellished cushions. A grand piano. Some polished silver candlesticks. That's all. Oh, and a pair of porcelain urns to flank the fireplace.

Visionaries' needs aren't exactly simple. But underlying their taste for opulence is a strong desire to create beauty that's rooted in tradition. Architecture plays an important role: Visionaries crave high ceilings and such details as crown molding, casement windows, and built-in bookcases. Plain, boxy living rooms with undistinguished features are enough to make a Visionary cry, but with energy, imagination, and a certain amount of money, even a prefab space can be transformed into a Visionary vision.

HOW TO TURN AN ORDINARY LIVING ROOM INTO A VISIONARY LIVING ROOM

- Install chair rails, crown molding, and a ceiling rosette.
- Paint the trim, the ceiling, and the walls below the chair rail in a cream-colored semigloss; paint the rest of the walls in a flat finish the exact color of Cabernet Sauvignon.
- If the room lacks a fireplace, install a decorative mantel. If the mantel needs painting, use the creamy trim color.
- Go crazy with drapery. Use fancy rods and tiebacks; combine heavy outer drapes with gauzy or lacy inner drapes.
- Install one large Oriental carpet lengthwise in the seating area and one small Oriental carpet crosswise in front of the mantel area.
- Choose classic or antique furnishings. Try to balance delicate pieces (carved spider-back chairs) with heavy pieces (overstuffed club chairs).
- Choose lamps with dark or richly colored shades.
- Create two wall arrangements that combine gilt-framed paintings, mirrors, sconces, and at least one surprise element such as an antique horse brass, a violin, or mounted butterflies. Hang groupings no higher than eye level.

The Artisan Living Room

Comfort and joy dwell in the Artisan's living room. With deep sofas, wide-open windows, fresh flowers, and plenty of cushions, Artisans can loll and lounge there to their hearts' content. Or, with tea and cupcakes set out on a painted tray, they can entertain friends. Or, with feet on an ottoman and Sunday papers all over the floor, they can bask in the privacy of early morning.

Artisan expression takes many forms. There is, at one extreme, the Artisan who admires the simple lines of rustic or primitive structures. Such an Artisan might have a living room in which stark vignettes—a straight-back chair against a brick wall, for instance—make the statement. At the other extreme are those Artisans who fill their living rooms with cushy love seats, painted chests, intriguing artifacts, and treasured mementos. Both styles combine a light touch, an understanding of texture, and a fondness for natural materials.

"Soft" is a key word in the Artisan design vocabulary. Colors are tempered, and shapes—though they may be strong of shoulder and broad of base—have rounded edges or are stooped with age. Surfaces are softened by texture; Artisans are attracted to that which is crackled, stressed, mottled, dappled, or napped. From floor to ceiling, the Artisan living room is easy on the eye.

THE ARTISAN VERSUS BALD WALLS

Artisans who live in new houses may be overwhelmed by the barren look of long, featureless living room walls. What do you do with miles of plain Sheetrock?

• Using a wide spackling knife, cover the walls with joint compound. Be speedy and messy, leaving visible swipes of the knife. When dry, sand gently; then cover with a wash of bright paint (buttery yellow, terra-cotta, goldenrod) cut with 50 percent water. Apply the paint quickly with a large brush. Voilà! Atmospheric, soulful stucco walls.

• Find two old windows—the larger the better—at a rummage sale or architectural salvage center. Tuck dried flowers, branches, and postcards behind the panes. Hang them side by side where you wish real windows were.

• Place a sofa against the longest wall and flank it with tall, deep bookshelves. This will create a nook effect, turning the cold expanse into an intimate seating area.

The Idealist Living Room

The Idealist living room makes a statement. It's strong and lean, pared down to the cleanest lines and the broadest sweeps of architecture. Le Corbusier's dream of a "machine for living" finds its fulfillment here; nothing is superfluous, and luxury is expressed not by decorative tchotchkes but by the integrity of good design.

This doesn't mean the Idealist living room is without a sense of fun. A wet bar tucked behind a hidden panel is very Idealist, designed to be revealed with a sly wink. A system of discreet speakers tucks jazz into every corner. Motion-sensitive lighting lends a dash of 007.

When choosing furniture, Idealists lean toward modern styles. Modular sofas may wind their way across vast floors, accompanied by chrome-and-leather chairs and sculptural tables; in the background there may be simple planes and powerful paintings, well kept and beautifully lit. The best Idealist living rooms are sophisticated and curiously serene, inviting gatherings that range from mobbed soirees to romantic tête-à-têtes.

A SENSE OF PLAY

Though Idealists have minimalist tendencies when it comes to architecture and furnishings, they love to puncture the sobriety of a room with gadgets, toys, visual puns, and unexpected witticisms. Don't be surprised to find any of the following in an Idealist dwelling:

- a phone booth
- fossils
- a jukebox
- an elaborate aquarium
- exotic birds
- Egyptian artifacts
- kinetic art
- oversize mobiles, not necessarily by Calder
- models of cars, planes, buildings, and dinosaurs

Pure space, filled with thoughts rather than things, is good for the soul. —DORIS SAATCHI

The Adventurer Living Room

The Adventurer living room is a feast for all the senses. More than a place to entertain, it is, in itself, entertaining.

It is in the Adventurer nature to get carried away—in fact, many Adventurers pride themselves on it—and their rooms are often a mad mix of color, concept, fantasy, and drama. And yet, though they come in all shapes and sizes, successful Adventurer living rooms have one thing in common: good flow. Few things are deadlier to Adventurous hosts than a dead-end room that makes visitors flop down and never move. One way they accomplish good flow is by grouping furni-

ture in the center of the room in a sort of conversation pit. This defines a center of action and allows constant movement along the outskirts; it also allows guests to get up and walk around without becoming the center of attention.

HOW TO FREE YOUR INNER ADVENTURER

If you're oppressed by other people's nations of good taste, maybe it's time to ignore your inner traditionalist and wake up your inner Adventurer. Some ideas to get you started:

• Think of your living room as a stage set. What would you like to see enacted there? *A Midsummer Night's Dream*? *The King and I*? *Madame Butterfly*? *The Rocky Horror Show*? Let your imagination loose on all of Hollywood, Broadway, opera, and beyond.

• Choose a favorite era and play it out in your decor. A swingin' sixties Burt Bacharach interior, for example, might feature plush upholstery in neon colors, shag carpeting, a well-preserved hi-fi, and a couple of beanbag chairs.

• Think United Nations. Combine artifacts, furnishings, and fabrics from countries all over the world. The look will stay harmonious if you follow a predetermined color scheme—vermilion, blue, and gold, perhaps.

TO SLEEP, PERCHANCE to dream . . . or perchance to read books, watch videos, get dressed, get naked, snuggle, sniffle, snore.

The bedroom is our personal oasis of comfort and privacy. It's the last place we see each night and the first place we sense upon our vulnerable first waking. It's also, more importantly, the one room in the house we can truly call our own, where we can shut the door and make the world go away.

All of us have our favorite sleeping quarters. The Visionary may crave a grand canopy bed in a well-appointed room (extra points if it's in a hotel), while the Artisan may shun such splendor and instead yearn for a hammock on the porch of a breezy oceanside cottage. The Idealist may feel happiest in the ultra-efficient space of a ship's cabin; the Adventurer might dream best on a huge mattress in a sleeping loft.

Whether we choose a tiny attic room or a luxurious suite, a well-considered bedroom can make us look forward to our nighttime retreat and give us something wonderful to wake up to.

The Bedroom

The Visionary Bedroom

For the intensely private Visionary, the bedroom is perhaps the most important room in the house. And within that room the most important piece is the bed itself. It determines the tone, direction, and layout of the space and should be selected and positioned before any other bedroom furnishing is considered.

Visionaries like the secure feeling of a framework, so it follows that they're happiest with canopy beds, four-poster beds, sleigh beds, or any bed that places them within a secure, strongly determined framework.

When it comes to bedroom storage, Visionaries should choose traditional or antique furniture that specifically suits their needs. Vanities, bureaus, jewelry chests, lingerie chests, and armoires can contribute to a rich, polished look that has the hush of quality. The Visionary's night table should have drawers or doors, so that it can double as a place to stash books, videos, and magazines; bed linens should be of the highest quality; windows should be dressed so as to block out light, or be pushed aside to let in the morning sun. Bed trays, blanket trunks, reading lamps, cushy carpets—all these items place the Visionary in the lap of luxury, and all have a place in the Visionary's bedroom.

YOURS, MINE, AND OURS

Lots of Visionaries require private time in bed to read, write letters, do crossword puzzles, or just think. This precious quietude can be compromised by the presence of a partner and could lead to tricky territorial issues. One solution: get two beds. Not twin beds à la Ricky and Lucy, but two large, beautiful beds that each partner can claim as his or her own and then abandon when it's time to snuggle up.

The Artisan Bedroom

The Artisans' favorite moment of the morning—and perhaps the whole day—is the slow second in which their eyes flutter open to a room bathed in sunlight.

It is this glorious moment that the Artisan anticipates and promotes. With bright white linens, windows dressed in bits of lace, polished floors, and simple furnishings, the best Artisan bedroom is a light-catcher that welcomes the sun.

It is also a place of comfort. Artisans love the silky feeling of cotton sheets that have been washed a thousand times, and the soulful presence of an antique quilt that whispers ancestral stories. In the bedroom the nature-loving Artisan wants to be lazy and pampered, surrounded by the soft smell of fresh laundry, the warmth of flannel, and the coolness of a tall glass of spring water.

Artisans should always choose furnishings that speak to them. A battered bassinet may become their favorite place to stash pajamas; jewelry may be stored in a collection of old tins. Who cares if that rug is falling to pieces? If it belonged to your grandmother and it means the world to you, let your feet fall upon it each morning. Sentiment, memory, and comfort come together where an Artisan rests.

REMEMBRANCES OF THINGS PAST

Many Artisans feel a need to be connected to the past. In seeking a sense of continuity and belonging, they may enshrine mementos that are infused with memories. A collection of brooches worn by an aunt, a one-eyed bunny rabbit saved since childhood, letters written by a long-dead grandfather—these touchstones remind the Artisan that he or she has a place in the world. And it is most often the bedroom where these treasures are kept, either on display in a place of honor or shuttered away in a very secret space.

The Idealist Bedroom

In the movie *9½ Weeks,* Mickey Rourke's character lives in an elegant loft furnished with Modernist museum pieces. Snooping through the apartment one day, his love slave—played by Kim Basinger—opens his closet door. There, hung in pristine, military order, are a dozen identical black suits. It is a surprising moment of beautiful minimalism. Forget the sex scenes; a peek into that closet is what makes the Idealist gasp with pleasure.

If Idealists had their way, their bedrooms would be professionally designed down to the last detail, and much of that attention would be given to solving the problem of storing personal effects. In their dreams, Idealists imagine closets in which outfits move on a motorized track, every pair of shoes is easily found and safe from dust, and each sweater has a sweater box. But the perfect closet doesn't *have* to be a dream. There are companies that specialize in storage solutions; they make house calls, assess clients' belongings, and custom-design closets that neatly house everything from parkas to pomade. Idealists on a budget can get the same effect by employing wardrobe racks, wire bins, and transparent boxes.

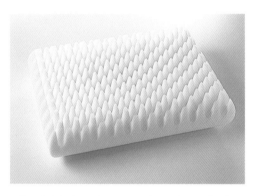

Once all of the unmentionables are in their place, Idealists ask little else of a bedroom. Give them a streamlined bed with access to an alarm clock, a telephone, and light switches. Keep the color palate pale and low in contrast. Then let the serene open space do the rest. Surrounded by quiet order, Idealists will sleep well.

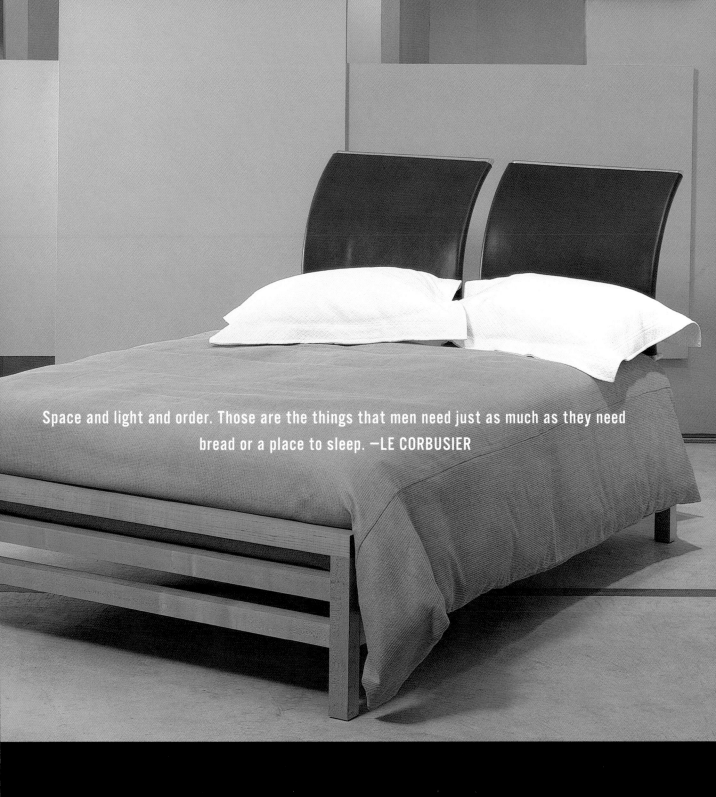

Space and light and order. Those are the things that men need just as much as they need bread or a place to sleep. —LE CORBUSIER

What You Might Find in an Idealist's Closet

An electric shoe polisher

Garment bags

A hanging jewelry organizer

A hanging belt organizer

An electric sweater-fuzz remover

Stacks of shoe boxes tagged with

Polaroid photographs of the

shoes inside

The Adventurer Bedroom

Every corner of the Adventurer's dwelling is lit up with personality. In the bedroom, it is the more intimate details of life that are put on parade. Their love for color and texture prompts Adventurers to set out small armies of bottled scents on the vanity, to stack carved boxes of jewels on the bureau, to stick festive postcards and photos in the corners of mirrors. Adventurers don't like shutting things away in drawers or closets, and often choose to drape their favorite accessories—scarves, neckties, strings of beads—on lampshades, hat stands, or the backs of chairs.

Adventurers' homes are fascinating to look at, but they nearly always teeter between order and chaos. Since Adventurers tend to be entirely uninterested in housework, their greatest challenge in the bedroom—indeed, in the whole house—is to maintain a sense of surprise and yet keep the room from looking like the aftermath of an explosion.

HOW TO KEEP CHAOS AT BAY

- Establish overall visual order by painting walls in a single, strong color.

- Use a very few large pieces of furniture, arranged with plenty of open space to provide breathing room for the eye. Once you have established a unifying background (the walls) and a well-defined middle ground (the furniture), the stage will be set for displays of personal effects.

- If you feel the need to put fifty-two necklaces on display, use a dozen identical hooks lined up on a wall. The different lengths and textures of the jewelry will keep things interesting, while the orderliness of the hooks will keep things neat. You can use the same trick for neckties, scarves, and belts.

- Stray perfume bottles, clutches, brushes, and candles will become a single choir when you group them on a tray or in an open box.

- Though they may seem very Idealist (and they are), closet organizers can do wonders for you, too. Shelves, racks, and cubbyholes will help you keep things organized, but also allow you to see everything at once, which is just how Adventurers like it.

The Kitchen

WHO IS INDIFFERENT toward the kitchen? It's the laboratory of the home, a place of alchemy where heat and moisture come together to provide sustenance. It's also where appliances gang up, messes get made, sharp tools are stored out of reach, and canned goods are stockpiled in case of flood or famine. And it's the place where everyone ends up clustering at parties.

In a home with an open floor plan, the dining area might flow into the living area, which in turn might dissolve into a family room. But the kitchen is always the kitchen, solidly in place and ready to fulfill the need for food, comfort, and company.

What is the kitchen's most powerful attraction? Sensual Visionaries love its sights and smells; for Artisans it is the sentimental center of home. Idealists believe a kitchen is only as good as its equipment, while high-spirited Adventurers think it's only as good as the good times one can have in it.

WHAT DO YOU THINK OF WHEN YOU THINK "KITCHEN"?

Visionary: Beauty

Artisan: Love

Idealist: Utility

Adventurer: Fun

The Visionary Kitchen

Visionaries revel in the kitchen's aesthetic opportunities; massive cabinets, fine hardware, and custom fixtures are just the beginning. Visionaries are likely to stock their pantries with attractively packaged imported goods and bottled water bubbling in colored glass. Wine racks are de rigueur; even the spices in the Visionary's cabinets are apt to be gorgeous. In short, the Visionary is anything but kitcheny.

The sensual pleasures of food are entirely seductive to most Visionaries. They approach cooking as an art, and, like most artists, they prefer to work alone and without pressure. Visionaries may spend days leafing through cookbooks or browsing through markets before rolling up their sleeves and making a meal.

Even when Visionaries aren't cooking, they pay attention to the presentation of food. Chinese take-out is made special when it's served on glazed plates with lacquered chopsticks. Pasta from the corner market tastes better in painted bowls with imported cheese. The way to a Visionary's heart is not just through the stomach; much depends on visuals.

COOKING WITH THE VISIONARY

Every gourmet Visionary should own:

• Cookbooks—especially hardcovers with lavish photographs

• An entire set of very good cookware

• Generous cabinets that hide unattractive pots and pans and reveal attractive plates and glassware

• Major appliances disguised as fine cabinetry

• A complete professional-quality cake-decorating set

• Accessories such as a fish poacher, gravy boat, trifle bowl, and asparagus tongs

The Artisan Kitchen

If the Artisan's kitchen table could talk, it would report on coffee breaks with friends, intimate suppers *à deux*, cookies decorated, beer consumed, letters written, taxes calculated, broken hearts mended. The kitchen is the soul of the Artisan's dwelling, and the kitchen table is where everything happens.

Why are Artisans most at home in the kitchen? Because they are connected to the rhythms of life. You can see this by what's in their kitchens (drying herbs, ripening tomatoes) and by what's missing (food processors, cappuccino machines, microwave ovens*).

Artisans don't seek convenience. They trust what is closest to the earth, and would rather do things the old-fashioned way. They're careful to hide anything plastic (recycling bins and cleaning products), and instead display rush-seat chairs, cotton dish towels, handmade bowls, and twig baskets. But the most important ingredients for a great Artisan kitchen include a screen door to a backyard, big windows, and the company of loved ones.

A minimum of two children is required before an Artisan will break down and buy a microwave oven.

THE MAKING OF A COUNTRY KITCHEN

Artisans love the wide-open spaces and rustic feeling of country kitchens. Some prefer kitchens that celebrate primitive Americana; others are partial to kitchens that evoke the countrysides of Tuscany and Provence. So how do city-dwellers lend country charm to a utilitarian space? Details can make all the difference.

• Use old milk bottles to hold fresh flowers. If you can find a half-dozen bottles in their original wooden carrier, a spray of blossoms in each makes a delightful display.

• Use galvanized buckets—available at hardware stores—to hold kitchen utensils.

• Old metal milk boxes make great bread boxes, and so do vintage ice chests.

• Thick butcher-block countertops can be bought by the foot and placed right on top of your existing counters.

• Terra-cotta pots are available in an enormous array of sizes and can serve not only as attractive containers, but also as organizers on shelves and in pantries.

• Wooden clothes pins can seal bags just like any "chip clip," keep stacks of paper bags in order, hold cookbooks open, clasp bunches of herbs together . . . and they always lend a nostalgic, countrified look.

The Idealist Kitchen

There are two kinds of Idealists: those who use the kitchen as a place to make things hot or make things cold, and those who use it as a place to make magic. The former type would be well advised to keep their kitchens as sparse and easy-to-clean as possible. The latter type should take out a bank loan and equip their kitchens with the best of everything.

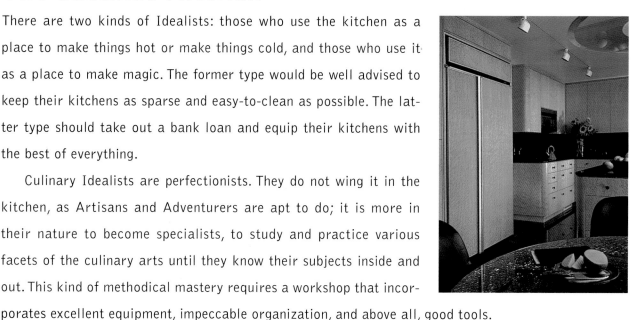

Culinary Idealists are perfectionists. They do not wing it in the kitchen, as Artisans and Adventurers are apt to do; it is more in their nature to become specialists, to study and practice various facets of the culinary arts until they know their subjects inside and out. This kind of methodical mastery requires a workshop that incorporates excellent equipment, impeccable organization, and above all, good tools.

Few things thrill the Idealist like using the right tool for the right job. If this means stocking the kitchen with egg slicers, strawberry corers, and french fry cutters, so be it. A professional-quality stove and refrigerator, which could seem wildly extravagant by other people's standards, may be a necessary element of the Idealist's culinary success.

Organization is also a priority. Idealists will most likely set up a logical system in the kitchen, so that big things (sinks and countertops) and small things (blenders and pounders and pepper grinders) are right where they're needed, when they're needed. And when the meal is done, the Idealist likes surfaces that are easy to clean, and cleaning equipment that gets the job done the *first* time.

THINGS YOU'LL NEVER FIND IN AN IDEALIST'S KITCHEN

Dull knives

Flawed or outdated appliances

Poor lighting

Unmatched flatware

Cut-rate ingredients

Unwashed dishes

Water-spotted glassware

Meddlers

I like the dreams of the future better than the history of the past. —THOMAS JEFFERSON

The Adventurer Kitchen

You'll never catch an Adventurer shooing a helpful guest out of the kitchen. To the Adventurer, cooking is a social activity and the kitchen is open to all visitors. Adventurers are party-givers, and the kitchen is where they bustle around, filling glasses, whipping up dishes, and mixing their work with big dollops of play.

Adventurer kitchen decor is always colorful. They're attracted to countertops in any shade but beige, brightly patterned plates, and walls hung with anything from chili-pepper lights to mounted marlins.

Because Adventurers couldn't care less about practicality, they tend to buy things simply because they like them, and so their kitchens are sometimes oddly equipped. A peek into their cabinets might reveal three hand-hammered woks and not one decent saucepan.

This same spirit of nonconformity can be seen in the Adventurer's cooking style. Rather than follow recipes, Adventurers are likely to riff, experiment, and invent dishes, often with fascinating results.

DELIGHT IN DISORDER

God help the stranger who attempts to cook in an Adventurer's kitchen. Quite unlike the organized Idealist, the Adventurer will subvert the intended use of just about any vessel. Looking for pasta? Try the cookie jar. Can't find a spatula? It might be in the champagne bucket, along with the soup ladle. If you intend to house-sit for an Adventurer, here's a tip: get a thorough Cook's tour first.

The Dining Room

THE INTUITIVE DINNER PARTY

Visionary: A catered sit-down dinner with multiple courses

Artisan: A picnic on a grassy hillside

Idealist: An ethnic meal with authentic accoutrements

Adventurer: A fascinating buffet featuring foods from around the globe to be sampled while socializing

DO YOU REMEMBER when every new American home had a dining room? Distinctly different from the kitchen, that noisy place of high chairs and breakfasts, the dining room was where grown-ups wore good clothes and conversed over candlelight. With a leaf or two added to the table, it was also where extended families converged for holiday dinners.

Today the line between kitchen and dining room has been blurred. Often a single table does triple duty: it's a place for casual suppers on the run and for fancier dinners with company; between meals it's a makeshift desk. In such circumstances it's not the room or the furniture that separates the kitchen from the dining area; it's the nuances of table settings and lighting.

Still, there are those who are lucky enough to have a proper dining room, separate and distinct. More than a mere place to eat, as the kitchen might be, the dining room is where significant rituals take place. There the ancient act of breaking bread is reenacted among ancestral trappings; prayers are said, candles are lighted, and everyone shares in a single feast. The whole concept of community is formalized and honored when people come together to dine.

The Visionary Dining Room

Because Visionaries value history, tradition, and ritual, everything about a formal dining room appeals to them. Fine old china, beautiful linens, candelabra, and voluptuous flower arrangements align with the Visionary aesthetic sense. Visionaries love the intimate theater of the dining table and often derive more pleasure from the place settings than from the dinner itself.

When Visionaries entertain, they may go all out with place cards, wine-specific stemware, and perfectly correct silverware and china, right down to the fish fork and the finger bowl. But it is the ritual of dining, above all else, that speaks to the Visionary soul. Even in compromised circumstances—say, during renovations, when the walls are stripped, the furniture's stored, and everything's covered in sawdust—the Visionary can turn dining into a special event. With a tarp as a tablecloth and a board as a table, the Visionary will light a candle and sup in style.

WHAT NOT TO DO WHEN DINING AT A VISIONARY'S HOME

- Do not suggest turning on the TV to watch the game during dinner.
- Do not invite extra guests along at the last minute.
- Do not saw your dinner roll in half to make a butter sandwich.
- Do not bring a six-pack of beer and pop open a can at the table.
- Don't plop down your beeper, cellular phone, cigarettes, and lighter next to your place setting.
- Don't assume your help in the kitchen is welcome.
- Do not ask for a toothpick after dinner.
- Do not assume a healthy belch conveys appreciation of a good meal.
- Do not attempt to stack all dishes in order to make just one trip to the kitchen.
- If asked to give a blessing, do not yell, "Rub-a-dub-dub, thanks for the grub, Yaaay, God!"

The Artisan Dining Room

Artisans are casual people who can be perfectly happy with one big all-purpose eating room. Those Artisans who are blessed with a dining room, however, will make great use of it. Many family-centered Artisans have a strong belief in the healing power of dinner; they work hard to bring everybody to the table all at once. Artisans want everyone to engage in conversation, enjoy nutritious meals, and tell their tales together.

Nothing is stiff or precious in the Artisan dining room. The Artisan host makes guests feel right at home; children are welcome, and rules about the correct fork and proper napkin placement are generally ignored. At holiday times Artisans can find themselves with a huge number of guests. It is on these occasions, when the old and the young are gathered together in celebration, that Artisans find profound joy.

THE SUMMERTIME ARTISAN

As soon as flowers start to bloom in the spring, the Artisan abandons the dining room and heads outdoors. Gatherings shift into laid-back affairs with loose timetables and picnic benches or blankets instead of chairs. The Artisan remains at the center of it all, bringing people together in the name of hot dogs, potato salad, watermelon, and long, balmy days. Those Artisans who lack yards somehow find a way to enjoy the summery months: you can spy them on rooftops, decks, porches, beaches and in public parks, sustained by good food and good weather.

After a good dinner one can forgive anybody, even one's own relatives. —OSCAR WILDE

The Idealist Dining Room

Idealists are not sentimental, nor are they driven by a need for ritual, but that doesn't mean they don't love dinner. When Idealists throw themselves into the task of entertaining, they can create evenings of seamless perfection. An Idealist wine dinner might feature exquisite vintages, each served at a precise temperature in the correct wineglass; a Japanese-themed dinner will no doubt include lacquered Japanese (not Chinese) chopsticks and sushi made with authentic ingredients, probably by a Japanese sushi chef hired for the occasion.

Idealists don't slap dinners together, mix culinary metaphors, or hastily create atmosphere. They want to do things right or not at all; for them, careful planning and research are half the fun.

In day-to-day life, Idealists tend to have personal rules regarding mealtimes. These rules may have to do with what time they eat, what foods they eat, or what can or cannot happen at the dinner table. In many Idealist households, the dining room is not used all that often, chiefly because life is too hectic or unpredictable for proper dinners. But when it is used, Idealists are likely to put forth feasts that are perfectly conceived and executed, from soup to Sambuca.

THE IDEALIST AS SPECIALIST

An Idealist who can't master all of cookery, or even a subgenre of cookery, might settle for perfecting one or two dishes. These specialties might be low-key (popovers from scratch) or wildly ambitious (flawless chateaubriand for twenty). Some Idealists master a single cooking process; grilling is a favorite. Consider the Idealistic appeal of the barbecue. It requires advance preparation, specialized equipment, use-specific tools, and easy cleanup. Such self-contained efficiency delights the Idealist through and through.

Life itself is the proper binge. —JULIA CHILD

The Adventurer Dining Room

The ever-festive Adventurer believes that life is to be lived, the good dishes are to be used, and the dining room shouldn't be saved for special occasions. In the Adventurer household, the dining room is likely to function as a breakfast nook, a sewing center, or a bingo parlor—that is, when there is not a marvelous dinner being enjoyed by an eclectic group of friends.

WHAT TO DO IF AN ADVENTURER
INVITES YOU TO DINNER

• Arrive late. Fifteen minutes is minimum.

• Before leaving home, call and ask if your host/hostess needs anything. Don't be surprised if you're sent on a mission for ice, shiitake mushrooms, or poker chips.

• Wear something wonderful.

• If you're asked to bring a bottle of wine, bring two.

• Anticipate lots of social time before dinner's served. If you're really hungry, consider snacking before you arrive.

• Understand that Adventurers love to experiment in the kitchen, so you may get a fabulous meal or a spectacular failure.

• Pitch in. Offer to clear tables, wash dishes, wipe counters.

• Be a sport. You might be cajoled into playing charades or a video game; go with the flow.

• Unless you get strong signals that your hosts are tired, stay longer than Amy Vanderbilt would ever recommend.

Adventurers have a knack for turning even the simplest supper into a party. It doesn't matter if the Adventurer has one dollar in the bank and is serving plain pasta; for richer or poorer, Drama is the Adventurer's middle name. You can be sure that dinner will be entertaining—but don't assume it will be served in the dining room. Adventurers are just as likely to have family and friends sit on the living room floor, in the kitchen, at a table in a rooftop garden, or around a campfire. Walls, tables, and designated dining areas can never enclose the Adventurer imagination.

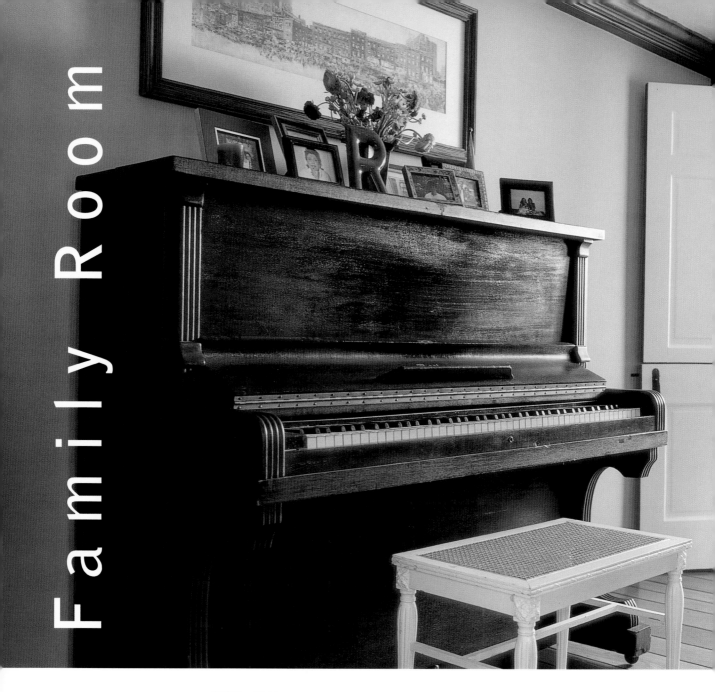

The Family Room

THE FAMILY ROOM, A.K.A. . . . .

Visionary	the sitting room
Artisan	the den
Idealist	the TV room
Adventurer	the rumpus room

WHAT IS A family room? It can be almost anything. The term itself is a vague, catch-all phrase that seems to have been coined because "the room that's less formal than the living room and is where people often watch television" was too long.

In fact, family rooms came into vogue at about the same time that television took America by storm. Since then, home entertainment has gotten considerably more complicated, and now the family room is where the members of the household gather to play video games and to watch the evening news, Saturday morning cartoons, and rented movies as well as to endure repeated viewings of Uncle Brad's disastrous ninetieth birthday party, caught on tape. It's also, more often than not, the place where audiotapes, CDs, and even the occasional record are played.

Of course, not all households are mediacentric, and not all family rooms are stuffed with equipment (many aren't stuffed with families, either). When you take away the entertainment systems, the family room is still a place to drop everything, stretch out, and enjoy some toes-up time, as the British say. So perhaps "family room" really means "the one area of the home that's dedicated to glorious downtime." Maybe we should just call it the playroom.

The Visionary Family Room

Visionaries need beauty and balance in their homes. So what do they do about unruly children, pets, sports-watching spouses, and an occasional urge to break out a bag of chips and watch the tube? You guessed it! They make themselves a cozy, comfy family room.

In the Visionary dwelling, the family room is usually located in a remote part of the home—or at least in an area that can be closed off by doors. It's where games are played (or watched), naps are taken, and teen slumber parties are held, but it's also very much a backstage area, meant to be kept out of sight of dinner guests and first dates.

Many Visionaries abhor the sight and sound of a television in an otherwise civilized room. These Visionaries, especially if they live alone or with a like-minded mate, might opt to set up a TV room in a spare bedroom. Then they'll use the family room as a place to read, listen to music, do needlepoint, or curl up by a fire.

No matter what the size and shape of the Visionary family room, it is likely to look quite different from the rest of the house. This is a room where standards are relaxed, where furniture can be stretched out on, coffee tables can be cluttered with late-night snacks, and shoes are optional.

A VISIONARY MUST-HAVE

Where families or familylike groups dwell together, it's nearly impossible to design a family room without incorporating a TV, VCR, and stereo. In fact, these electronics often become the focal point of the family room, much to the chagrin of the Visionary. Rather than fighting this reality, however, the Visionary might consider investing in a cabinet that houses an entertainment system. The best of these units are self-contained; when closed, they masquerade as attractive cabinetry. Such pieces go a long way toward restoring a room's dignity at the end of the day.

The Artisan Family Room

To the Artisan, virtually every room is a family room. So when it comes to decorating that area of the home, Artisans shine. As dedicated creatures of comfort, they know exactly how to make a family room that's inviting and relaxing.

Like Visionaries, Artisans can be sensitive to the buzz and blare of electronics. But they also tend to indulge other people's pleasures, even to the point of allowing giant, puffy recliners and modern entertainment centers into their homes.

Except for these concessions, the Artisan family room is only slightly different from the living room. Furniture may be better able to survive scuffs and spills; cushions may be oversize so that they can be scattered on the floor; and rugs may be extra-thick in order to accommodate toddlers, cats, and aerobic workouts.

WHAT ARTISANS KEEP IN THEIR FAMILY ROOMS:

Afghans

Photo albums

Toy chests

Foot massagers

Knitting projects

Snack trays

Rocking chairs

Magazines

Board games

Yoga videos

Jigsaw puzzles

Books on tape

The Idealist Family Room

Idealists love systems. So how can a room that has a system at its center be anything but awesome? A wide-screen TV with on-screen programming, a powerful VCR, a 100-disc CD jukebox, a laser disc player, a full surround-sound system—these put the "wow" in the Idealist home. A state-of-the-art entertainment system provides the Idealist with education, communication, and fun at the push of a button.

Since nothing pleases Idealists more than showing off their technological toys, they will furnish the family room with inviting sofas, dimmer-switch lighting, comfy carpeting, an auxiliary refrigerator, and a whole library of discs and tapes—but only one remote control.

THE IDEALIST AND THE TUBE: A LOVE MATCH

Not all Idealists are enchanted by technology, but many of them are dedicated TV watchers. There are reasons for this. First, television itself is a reliable system. The shows may not be the greatest, but they are there, on time every day, each carefully formatted and soothingly predictable. This gives the Idealist a sense of continuity, and a feeling that things are running smoothly; as such, they find television extremely relaxing. Second, watching TV is a great pastime for neatniks. Idealists like the fact that a full evening's entertainment can be tidily contained in a small black box, with little or no cleanup required. And third, for those many Idealists who are information junkies, the TV is an ever-unfolding source of fresh news. They're likely to keep it on all day and night as a kind of background presence, glancing up now and then to check on stock prices, sports scores, or late breaking events.

My problem lies in reconciling my gross habits with my net income. —ERROL FLYNN

The Adventurer Family Room

Adventurers don't like single-task rooms. Which means they appreciate the open-ended possibilities that a family room affords. At the slightest suggestion Adventurers will move the family room furniture against the walls to make space for a limbo contest or a tai chi demonstration; they'll happily eat laptop meals while watching sitcoms, or they'll invite way too many people over to see a pay-per-view boxing match. Adventurers do best when their family rooms are outfitted with movable, easy-to-store furnishings, like TV trays, folding chairs, and card tables. Heavy recliners may be comfortable, but they'll eventually thwart the Adventurer's need for a flexible floor plan.

One exception to the "move it or lose it" rule is the convertible sofa. Adventurers love to have company, including overnight guests; in the Adventurer household, the family room often doubles as a guest room.

ADVENTURER ALTERNATIVES

Conventional family room furniture doesn't exactly make Adventurers' hearts go pitter-pat. But with imagination and a willingness to forage, the family room can become the wittiest room in the house. Some furnishings to consider:

• Rows of folding seats from an old movie theater
• Blow-up vinyl chairs and chaises
• Oversize bolsters that can be piled on the floor into sofa-like shapes
• Vintage beauty parlor chairs (with or without hairdryer bonnets)
• Coleman ice chests as end tables
• Welcome mats as area rugs
• Glass top coffee tables with bases made from mannequin parts, tires, canned goods, engine parts, or glass-enclosed dioramas of the Alamo, the Creature of the Black Lagoon, or Godzilla attacking New York

"HOME OFFICE" AS EUPHEMISM

When a co-worker announces that he or she will be spending the day working at home, don't be fooled into imagining a traditional home office. Though the IRS may or may not agree, any of the following could be a home office:

A sound stage	A garage full of tools	A sewing room
A potting shed	A dance floor	A laptop on the patio
A darkroom	A cubbyhole with a desk	The kitchen or dining
A home gym	and a phone	room table

THERE WAS A time, not so very long ago, when an ad for a three-bedroom house would automatically attract people with two children. These days more and more house-hunters call real estate agents and ask, "Will one of the bedrooms work as an office?"

Some 30 million Americans conduct business from the home, and that number increases daily. The personal computer started the work-at-home revolution, and when button-down types began trading their suits for bathrobes, the whole world took notice. But think about it: haven't people always worked at home, in one capacity or another?

The home office isn't always four walls and a Power Mac. But it *is* always a personal space where dreams are made real. Painters need their pigment-spattered studios; pianists need their practice rooms; woodworkers would be lost without their shops.

Home is a place for rest, sustenance, privacy, and love. And now, thanks to social evolution, it is also a playground for the mind and a boon to the bank account.

The Home Office

The Visionary Home Office

The term "home office" is a bit bald for the Visionary. It implies something as banal as commerce, and hints at unattractive electronic equipment clad in beige plastic. The Visionary prefers "library" or "study," words that suggest a room where books weigh heavily in polished cases. Visionaries love libraries—be they libraries of books, videos, CDs, or sheet music—and feel deeply contented when surrounded by a world of knowledge.

The ideal Visionary study is warm and hushed, protected from clamor by solid doors, heavy drapes, and thick carpets. Floor-to-ceiling bookshelves, preferably built in, function not only as storage but also as mufflers of sound.

Since Visionaries tend to be turned off by metal and plastic, most modern office furniture leaves them cold. They far prefer traditional-style furnishings that cleverly conceal equipment. A big leather chair would also suit the average Visionary, as would a divan for reading, reclining, and scheming.

ADVICE FOR THE WORK-AT-HOME VISIONARY

• Ignore modern desks topped with Formica or veneer. Shop for a traditional hardwood model, and remember: antique desks can be discreetly drilled to accommodate modern electrical cords.

• Reject metal filing cabinets. Go for oak, especially models that are disguised as chests of drawers.

• Hide from fluorescent lights. Choose table lamps for direct lighting and floor lamps for indirect lighting.

• Shun plastic trays and standing files. Use antique letter holders, letter boxes, and vintage newspaper racks.

• Don't buy fistfuls of plastic pens. Splurge instead on fine writing instruments that coordinate with your desk set. And don't scrimp on writing paper.

The Artisan Home Office

Why do Artisans love to work at home? Because they can show up at the office in their pajamas, sip coffee from a favorite mug, check the bird feeders, and bake bread while making business calls. Their office interiors are usually a bit scruffy, designed not for slick efficiency but for blessed inspiration.

Artisans, like Visionaries, tend to recoil from high-tech electronics. It's not just an aesthetic objection; Artisans cling to old reliable methods. Some even take pride in their resistance to technology and will peck out letters on an old Olivetti or refuse to replace their 10-pound rotary phone.

New office furniture is unappealing to Artisans. They're much happier when they can turn an old kitchen table into a desk, store papers and supplies in a painted chest of drawers, and surround themselves with photographs pinned on bulletin boards and pots jammed with pencils.

More important than furniture and equipment choices, however, is the physical space of the Artisan office. The bigger the windows, the happier an Artisan will be. It's pointless for any Artisan to consider working in a windowless office; it might as well be a prison cell. He or she will avoid it and set up temporary posts in sunny nooks elsewhere in the house.

THE ARTISAN'S FAVORITE
OFFICE SPACES

Barns with big sliding doors

Attics with exposed beams

Pool houses

Greenhouses

Atriums

Garrets

Groundskeepers' cabins

Tents

Cottages

Treehouses

Stables

Lighthouses

Houseboats

Beach houses

Huts

I don't really have studios. I wander around—around people's attics, out in fields, in cellars, anyplace I find that invites me. —ANDREW WYETH

The Idealist Home Office

Idealists are in love with the modern world, and nowhere is this romance more fulfilling than in the home office. Much of today's contemporary office furniture is made by Idealists *for* Idealists. Desks, storage units, lights, and especially chairs are not so much designed as engineered; every piece earns its keep, and the stripped-down aesthetic of office equipment is completely in line with the Idealist sensibility.

Idealists are creatures of logic. When planning a home office, business comes first: Idealists analyze their needs and then, after careful research, find the best tools for the job. Though it is equipment that informs the Idealist's office style, the results are often starkly beautiful. A simple color scheme—matte black, burnished aluminum—and the bare-bones silhouettes of industrial furniture can combine to create an environment that is both sleek and chic.

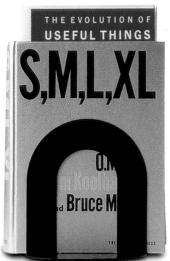

BABY, IT'S YOU

The newest work stations are an Idealist's dream. Much more than desks, they are furniture systems in which various components can be combined to suit the user. Choosing from among such options as hutches for monitors, shelves for printers, keyboard drawers, and filing cabinets on casters, home workers can custom-design a work area for themselves. Many furniture companies also offer coordinating bookshelves and credenzas, so the look can be carried throughout the office. Equipped with built-in cord organizers to keep bundles of cables out of sight, the new work stations go a long way toward the Idealist's goal of having a clean desk at the end of the day.

If A equals success, then the formula is A equals X plus Y plus Z. Y is play. Z is keep your mouth shut. —ALBERT EINSTEIN

The Adventurer Home Office

Adventurers are intellectual browsers who mentally leap through time and space to find grand connections between big ideas. So how does a person combine interests as varied as ballet, entomology, fine wines, anatomy, and the music of the Italian Renaissance? That's a question that Adventurers ask themselves all the time. It's not surprising that the average Adventurer work space looks like the hideaway of a mad anthropologist, layered with the fallout of past projects and a stockpile of future ambitions.

Certain pieces of equipment can help keep the Adventurer from being literally buried in work. A portable phone, for instance, allows the Adventurer to look for things while talking. Anything on casters is also useful. Adventurers should avoid stationary filing cabinets except for archival purposes; they simply don't have an *a*-to-*z* mentality and are likely to forget anything that's been put away. Their best organizational tools are bulletin boards and Post-it notes. Shelves can serve not only as display areas but also as storage for equipment, supplies, and books. With enough shelving, Adventurers may even curb their penchant for stacking stuff on floors, tables, and all other surfaces within reach.

STAND AND DELIVER

Since Adventurers need to spread out and keep moving, Adventurer offices should include at least one table—a credenza of sorts—that is waist high and well lighted. It is here, standing up, that the Adventurer will sign letters, look things up, and open mail. Lots of famous folks preferred to work standing up, including Thomas Wolfe, Winston Churchill, Ernest Hemingway, and Thomas Jefferson. Although it's not certain they were all Adventurers, they certainly made things happen.

The Bathroom

WHAT DO YOU DO IN THE TUB?

Visionary: read novels by candlelight.

Artisan: play with natural softening, exfoliating, or aromatherapy products.

Idealist: direct sore muscles toward whirlpool jets.

Adventurer: listen to music or talk on the phone while luxuriating in movie-star bubbles.

FOR SOME, THE bathroom is a steamy retreat. For others, it's a bright, clean cubicle briefly visited in the A.M. and the P.M. But whether you're a quick, efficient shower person (76 percent of Americans are) or a slow, dreamy bath person (as 28 percent of women and 22 percent of men claim to be), there's no disputing that, in terms of home design, the bathroom is small but mighty.

The most modern and extravagant of today's bathrooms feature separate areas for bathing, showering, toileting, and shaving or applying makeup. In the midcentury, however, the bathtub-shower, toilet, and sink were all together and all surrounded by coordinating tiles, usually in pastel tones. Earlier still, people enjoyed the kind of bathroom that Evelyn Waugh wrote about in *Brideshead Revisited*—a room that housed a "deep, copper, mahogany-framed bath that was filled by pulling a brass lever." He compared its welcoming warmth with the "clinical little chambers glittering with chromium-plate and looking-glass, which pass for luxury in the modern world."

Be it brand-new or positively Victorian, a well-designed bath can be a place of contentment as well as cleanliness.

The Visionary Bathroom

When a visitor confronts a Windsor chair, parlor-quality prints, and elaborate window treatments in a bathroom, it's certain they've entered a Visionary's domain. Creature comforts of the old-fashioned variety abound in this bath. Visionaries are partial to claw-footed tubs, pedestal sinks, graceful faucets, stacks of oversize towels, and beautiful bottles of this and that.

If a Visionary were forced to choose just two bath essentials, however, they would likely be (1) a door that locks and (2) an endless supply of hot water. Whether it's four-star fancy or boardinghouse plain, the Visionary bath is the perfect place to be naked and alone with fragrant steam and all the thoughts of the day.

BUILDING A BETTER VISIONARY BATHROOM

- Size matters. If you're a Visionary, a large bathroom is part of your happiness; keep this in mind when conversing with contractors or real estate agents.
- Get rid of overhead and fluorescent lights. Instead, install makeup lights around the mirror (sconces work well) and use table or floor lamps for general lighting.
- Any bathroom accessory that can be bought in a hardware store doesn't belong in a Visionary home. Forget run-of-the-mill medicine cabinets and prefab vanities; an old sideboard can be fitted with plumbing to accommodate a sink, while bureaus can hold towels and toiletries in high style.
- Visionaries thrive in warm, rich environments. So if you're stuck with a beige-tiled bathroom, get brave with dark paint and rugs. Use strongly patterned fabrics for curtains and shower curtains, and remember: a deep colored ceiling will warm even the coldest WC.

The Artisan Bathroom

Artisans care very much about their bodies. And for many Artisans, the bathroom is Body-Care Central. Lotions and potions (especially if they're herbal) and soaps and exfoliants (especially if they're organic) make Artisans feel good about the skin they're in.

A bathtub is essential Artisan equipment, even if it's used only on occasion. The bath ritual allows Artisans to reconnect with themselves: weightlessness and water lift away cares and lull Artisans

into a state of blissful meditation.

The best Artisan bathrooms are bright, open spaces softened by the textures of nature and the past. An old painted wooden chair, scented candles, moisture-loving plants, a bowl of natural sea sponges, and a bouquet of makeup brushes all look right at home in the Artisan bathroom.

THE ARTISAN AS EDITOR

Eliminate:	Replace with:
opaque or plastic shower curtains	lacy or gauzy shower curtains
window blinds	etched or frosted-glass windows
tiled floors	sisal floor covering
standard medicine cabinets	antique mirrors
plastic-handled scrubbers	wooden-handled scrubbers
aerosol or plug-in air fresheners	potpourri or incense

If you consider the contribution of plumbing to human life,
the other sciences fade into insignificance. —JAMES GORMAN

The Idealist Bathroom

Nozzles! Pipes! Tiles! Sprayers, drains, basins, faucets! Any Idealist with enough cash and space can have a fabulous time creating a dream bathroom. Cool gleaming surfaces, clean geometry, and great gadgets can all come together to make a high-tech spa in which to splash and play. Before shopping for fixtures, however, the Idealist should consider where all those aspirin bottles, blow dryers, cleaning products, and et ceteras will be stored. How about a mirror-clad, full-wall cabinet, a massive medicine chest (built in, natch),

and a sleek alcove in the shower stall?

Once they've selected their storage systems, Idealists should choose the shiniest, most multifunctional equipment possible. The antiseptic beauty of ceramic, porcelain, and advanced plumbing will keep them on the path of clean living.

WHAT IDEALISTS SHOULD HAVE IN THE BATHROOM

Walls clad in marble or glossy tiles

A shower stall with sliding glass doors

A digital bathroom scale

A magnifying mirror

A Water Pik

An exhaust fan

WHAT IDEALISTS WISH THEY HAD IN THE BATHROOM

A Jacuzzi

A towel heater

A waterproof telephone

A three-way mirror

Automatic soap and
    shampoo dispensers

A television set

A newspaper rack

The Adventurer Bathroom

Nobody can convince an Adventurer that rooms should be practical and efficient. The word "standard" barely exists in Adventurers' vocabulary; their personal dwellings are always filled with creative touches and surprises. The bathroom is no exception to this rule.

In terms of decorating, Adventurers like bathrooms because they're small, compact areas where personal statements can be made in a big way. If an Adventurer decides to festoon a transparent shower curtain with Band-Aids, so be it; if he or she covers the floor in AstroTurf, that's okay, too.

In the bathroom, Adventurers fully flex their talent for reappropriating objects. They will, for instance, employ a child's plastic sand bucket as a container for soaps, use a distributor cap as a toothbrush holder, and recruit saltine tins to hold cotton balls, Q-Tips, and disposable razors.

Guests might never leave.

WHAT YOU MIGHT FIND IN
AN ADVENTURER'S BATHROOM

A huge circus poster

Crocheted toilet paper dolls with big skirts

Shark oil and bay rum mixed in with normal
    medicine-cabinet items

Bubble bath decanted into champagne bottles

Shampoo meant for horses

Ointment meant for cows

A colorful selection of mismatched towels

Twenty-one shades of nail polish, all on display

Visionary

History, tradition, royalty. The Visionary loves the pageantry of gold, the significance of regal purple, the bloody beauty of crimson, the articulate splendor of aged linen. Quality colors, deep and dignified, enrich the Visionary's home.

Artisan

Spice, light, sweetness. Patina, pentimento, parchment. Colors and textures that speak of nature are in harmony with the Artisan spirit—and colors and textures made in a laboratory are banished.

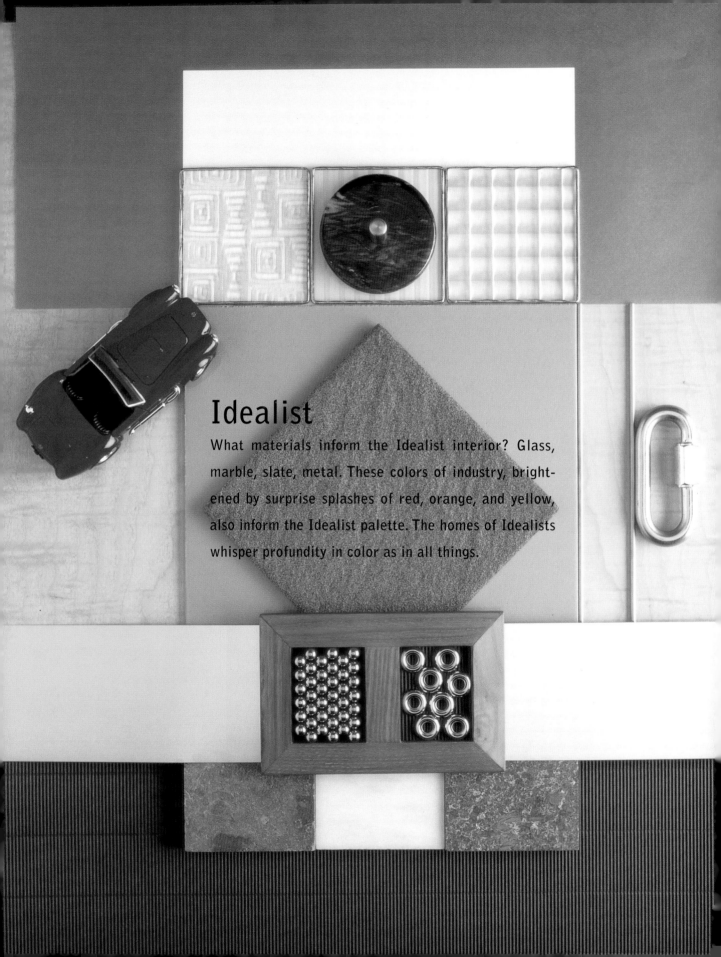

Idealist

What materials inform the Idealist interior? Glass, marble, slate, metal. These colors of industry, brightened by surprise splashes of red, orange, and yellow, also inform the Idealist palette. The homes of Idealists whisper profundity in color as in all things.

Adventurer

Mix bold patterns, Indian block prints, vivid silks, and bright batiks and what have you got? The Adventurer palette. Colors that lie oppo- site each other on the color wheel will suit Adventurers best, but any unexpected mix will thrill them just as much.

Windows

Complex, sensual **Visionaries** never allow their windows to be underdressed. Instead, they layer them with yards of luxurious fabric. Visionaries—who, let's not forget, are altar-builders—know exactly what to do with valances, rods, finials, tiebacks, swags, satin ropes, fringe, tassels and borders. Their window dressings are not only decorative: they provide Visionaries with barriers against the noise, light, chill, and heat of the outside world.

Artisans wish they didn't need curtains at all. They crave sunlight and moonbeams, the patter of rain and the blush of dawn. Where privacy or extreme weather isn't an issue, Artisans sometimes opt to dress their windows with diaphanous scarves as a dreamy, decorative way to soften the hard edges of architecture. Where drapery is demanded, Artisans choose curtains in the fabrics they love best: pure cottons, raw linens, and layers of lace.

Of the four archetypes, **Idealists** most appreciate the convenience and geometry of window blinds. This is especially true in rooms where windows are well positioned and therefore architecturally pleasing. But Idealists also have a way with intriguing materials, and may add unusual hardware, or replace clear window panes with glass bricks, or choose to disperse the morning light with free-standing shoji screens.

Adventurers like to invent their own design solutions. So it's unlikely they'd choose their window dressings from a curtain store. Instead, they might hang frosted vinyl shower curtains from metal hoops, or combine striped fabrics for a Bedouin tent effect, or cover panes of glass with colorful lighting gels, or make curtains from an Indian sari and tie them back with Mardi Gras beads.

Artisan

The Vertical Still Life

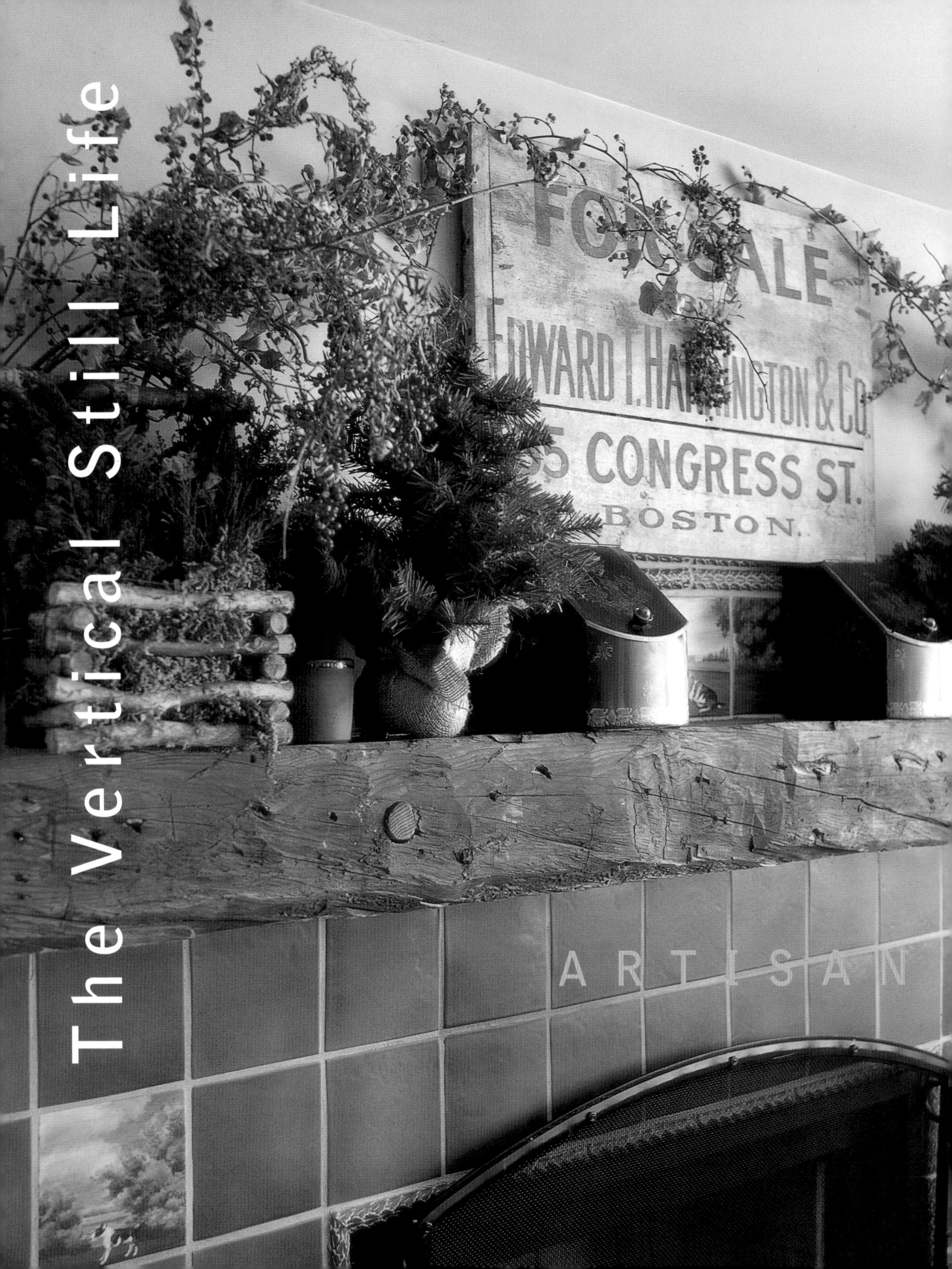

ARTISAN

Visionary

What do you have on your walls?

The **Visionary's** altar-building instincts translate into beautiful, balanced compositions. Renaissance sketches, fragments of classical architecture, Victorian posey-holders, sconces, and religious images can find a place on the Visionary's walls—and so can luscious, remarkable frames of all kinds. Whether sparse or delightfully dense, Visionary wall arrangements are rich displays of favorite things.

On the **Artisan's** walls, intriguing textures and subtle colors converge. Artisans are attracted to folk art—stitched samplers, rough-hewn carvings, primitive paintings, handmade tools—and when these items are combined with vines and weathered wood, the results are enchanting. The best Artisan arrangements, which are spare enough to let the wall "breathe," feature things that are not normally used for decoration: old paintbrushes, for instance, or a solitary leaf.

The sociable **Adventurer** loves dialogue—between people and also between objects. A gilded print of an Indian goddess might make a lovely hanging, but it is far more provocative when it's paired with scraps of paper typewritten with haiku, anchored with a glittering hatpin. Adventurers' walls are full of surprises, and each item plays off the others. Seemingly disparate forms, colors, patterns, textures, contexts, subtexts, and genres all frolic there together.

The **Idealist's** aesthetic is expressed on walls that celebrate what is not there as much as what is. Idealists use negative space to dramatic effect. A cathedral ceiling might be enhanced by a small painting hung near the rafters and nothing else. A massive tapestry may be the only decorative object in a room, and it will look all the more magnificent for its solitude. Such brave compositions require an unerring hand and eye, but this is the gift of the Idealist, for whom less is indeed more.

ADVENTURER

Storage

The **Visionary's** sense of order runs deep. Storage is not merely a way of hiding things from sight; the Visionary wants pieces that stand on their own as beautiful furnishings. Highboys, lowboys, breakfronts, curio cabinets, and secretaries all appeal to Visionaries, as do lingerie chests, cedar closets, and jewelry boxes. The ultimate Visionary piece is the glass-front china cabinet: the idea that precious keepsakes can be safely shuttered away while still in view is very much in the Visionary spirit.

Visionaries take their possessions seriously and tend to pamper them in every way. Therefore they often employ such old-fashioned niceties as drawer liners, sachets, and padded hangers. These help ensure that what is special will remain so for many years.

Artisans like to rescue old, abandoned pieces and give them new life in the home. Often these pieces were

Adventurer

Visionary

originally meant to be used for storage—think of Hoosier cabinets, hutches, steamer trunks, and hatboxes—but were never intended to make an appearance in the living room, bedroom, or bathroom. The Artisan makes them work wherever they're needed. Whether it's an old medicine chest stuffed with art supplies, an antique pharmacist's cabinet filled with spices, or a wooden fruit crate stacked with audiotapes, the Artisan has a talent for creative containment.

ARTISAN

STERS
CIPLES
OF THE
E MASTER

Idealists know that good storage is a science. It's an aspect of home design on which they will spend significant time and money, because they do not want the underthings of life cluttering countertops and tables. So Idealists plan carefully, considering what they've got and what they may have in the future.

Idealists prefer customized storage solutions. They like smooth-surfaced wall units, free of excess adornment; even the handles on an Idealist cabinet are likely to be slender and simple. Once those cabinets and closets are opened, however, the Idealist's genius for organization is revealed. No space is wasted, and everything, from paper clips to winter coats, has a place to live.

Adventurers have a storage paradox. They tend to own an excess of stuff; when the typical Adventurer stows something out of sight, however, it's instantly out of mind. Adventurers rely heavily on visual reminders of where their possessions can be found; to them, no object is an island, and a thing is defined by that which surrounds it.

Which is why pantries, CD towers, open shelves, hat racks, and hooks are all must-haves in the Adventurer household. For those situations in which Adventurers really do want things to disappear, closets and cabinets are good options, but they are less successful with bureaus. You know that classic comedy routine in which a frantic person rifles through drawers, tossing everything aside in a search for something important? That's pure Adventurer.

IDEALIST

...with Artisan tendencies, you might:
Fill a polished breakfront with a collection of flea market finds. (Visionaries have an affinity for displaying treasured items behind glass; Artisans treasure items that have been rescued from obscurity.)

If You're a Visionary...

...with a strong Idealist streak, you might:
Have brand-new thermal-paned windows installed in your home, then swathe them in heavy drapery. (Idealists make the most of modern technology, but Visionaries never pass up an opportunity to dress a window.)

...with liberal doses of Adventurer, you might:
Host formal dinner parties at the drop of a hat. (Adventurers love all kinds of spontaneous gatherings; Visionaries want everything to be just so, especially at the dinner table.)

Split

...with lots of Adventurer spirit, you might:
Display unusual groupings of knick-knacks—carved jungle animals, antique bocci balls—all in earth colors. (It's very Adventurer to juxtapose surprising items, and very Artisan to maintain a natural, earth-toned palette.)

...with an Idealist streak, you might:
Build an ultra-modern stable for your horses. (Artisans are hands-on animal lovers, while Idealists delight in high-tech environments.)

If You're an Artisan...

...with heavy Visionary tendencies, you might:
Live in a rambling country house and keep an apartment in the city. (Artisans are country mice; Visionaries are city mice.)

...with a Visionary streak, you might:
Install a remote-control fireplace fueled by gas jets. (Romantic Visionaries adore the ambience of a crackling fire. To the Idealist, the real fun is lighting it from across the room.)

...with Artisan tendencies, you might:
Have an indoor swimming pool. (Water-baby Artisans would relish a daily swim, while Idealists would prefer a daily swim in an environment where weather and insects were never an issue.)

If You're an Idealist...

...with Adventurer characteristics, you might:
Buy a high-end stereo system and tuck it inside an old hi-fi console. (Most Idealists insist on state-of-the-art digital sound, but witty Adventurers would enjoy disguising a new system as a clunky, out-of-date system.)

Personalities

...with strong Artisan tendencies, you might:
Display stacks of scented soaps in the bathroom, all in neon colors. (Bath products are some of the Artisan's favorite things, but they usually prefer all-natural soaps; Adventurers like accessories that offer some visual excitement.)

...with Visionary qualities, you might:
Buy a Limoges platter at auction, then fill it with unexpected objects—dog biscuits, for example, or a collection of vintage glass eyes. (Though Adventurers might be seduced by the beauty of Visionary-like items, such as Limoges platters, they're not likely to take them 100-percent seriously.)

If You're an Adventurer...

...with Idealist impulses, you might:
Have your bedroom closet professionally organized to accommodate your winter wardrobe, your summer wardrobe, and your entire collection of blue suede shoes. (Idealists insist on good organization in the home, but blue suede shoes would likely be collected by rock 'n' roll Adventurers.)

Resource Guide

Jacqueline Albanese
On the Fringe
Belmont, MA
Phone: (617) 782-2016

America Dural Interior
Architecture and Design
Phillip Jude Miller
359 Boylston Street,
Suite 505
Boston, MA 02166
Phone: (617) 267-1699
Fax: (617) 859-5815

Becker Designed, Inc.
14101 A Parke Long Court
Chantilly, VA 20151
Phone: (703) 803-6900
Fax: (703) 803-6903

Beverly Furniture
Manufacturing
Mike Moore
4859 Gregg Road
Pico Rivera, CA 90660
Phone: (310) 695-5721

Biomorph
Ground Support
Equipment (US) Ltd.
129 West 22nd Street
New York, NY 10011
Phone: (212) 647-9595
Fax: (212) 647-9596

Ted Boerner Furniture Design
10 Arkansas Street, Studio G
San Francisco, CA 94107
Phone: (415) 487-0110
Fax: (415) 487-0111

Agnes Bourne, Inc.
2 Henry Adams Street
Showroom 220
San Francisco, CA 94103
Phone: (415) 626-6883
Fax: (415) 626-2489

Bravo 20
Eric Pfeiffer
161 Natoma Street
San Francisco, CA 94105
Phone: (415) 495-3914
Fax: (415) 495-4678

Lauren Caldwell
81 Perry Street
New York, NY 10014
Phone: (212) 206-6959

Robert Clisby
RC Design
7071 Astoria Street
San Diego, CA 92111
Phone/Fax: (619) 277-6644

Directions Contract and
Residential Furnishings
195 East 200 North
Alpine, UT 84004
Phone: (801) 763-0954
Fax: (801) 756-0482

Domain Home Fashions
Executive Office
51 Morgan Drive
Norwood, MA 02062
Phone: (617) 769-9130
Fax: (617) 769-3580
www.intuitive-home.com

Domain store locations:

Danbury Fair Mall
7 Backus Avenue
Danbury, CT 06811
Phone: (203) 798-1299
Fax: (203) 798-0132

Milford
1422/1424 Boston Post Road
Milford, CT 06460
Phone: (203) 876-5045
Fax: (203) 226-8290

Stamford Town Center
100 Greyrock Place
Stamford, CT 06901
Phone: (203) 964-1643
Fax: (203) 357-0142

Westfarms Mall
66 Westfarms Mall, Suite 107
Farmington, CT 06032
Phone: (860) 561-4860
Fax: (860) 561-4322

Westport
3 Post Road East
Westport, CT 06880
Phone: (203) 226-8880
Fax: (203) 226-8290

Chevy Chase
5454 Wisconsin Avenue
Chevy Chase, MD 20815
Phone: (301) 652-0799
Fax: (301) 652-8832

Montgomery Mall
7107 Democracy Boulevard
Bethesda, MD 20817
Phone: (301) 365-8900
Fax: (301) 365-4410

Burlington Mall
Middlesex Turnpike
Burlington, MA 01803
Phone: (781) 273-2288
Fax: (781) 270-7975

The Mall at Chestnut Hill
199 Boylston Street
Chestnut Hill, MA 02167
Phone: (781) 964-6666
Fax: (781) 964-8976

Newbury Street
7 Newbury Street
Boston, MA 02116
Phone: (781) 266-5252
Fax: (781) 267-1894

Norwood Warehouse
51 Morgan Drive
Norwood, MA 02062
Phone: (781) 769-9130
Fax: (781) 769-3580

Bridgewater Commons
400 Commons Way,
Suite 139
Bridgewater, NJ 08807
Phone: (908) 707-9333
Fax: (908) 707-1576

Elizabeth Warehouse
c/o Domain, Inc.
720 South Front Street
Elizabeth, NJ 07202
Phone: (908) 354-5013
Fax: (908) 354-5014

Freehold Raceway Mall
3710 Route 9, Suite 1401
Freehold, NJ 07728
Phone: (732) 308-0303
Fax: (731) 308-9891

The Mall at Short Hills
Route 24 & JFK Parkway
Short Hills, NJ 07078-2799
Phone: (973) 379-9111
Fax: (973) 379-9158

Menlo Park Mall
397 Menlo Park
Edison, NJ 08837-4405
Phone: (732) 603-7300
Fax: (732) 603-5081

Paramus
290 Route 4 East
Paramus, NJ 08752
Phone: (201) 487-4222
Fax: (201) 487-3222

Hartsdale
112 South Central
Hartsdale, NY 10503
Phone: (914) 949-9022
Fax: (914) 949-9418

Manhasset
1516 Northern Boulevard
Manhasset, NY 11030
Phone: (516) 365-5533
Fax: (212) 639-1106

Manhattan
938 Broadway
(at 22nd Street)
New York, NY 10010
Phone: (212) 228-7450
Fax: (212) 228-8591

Roosevelt Field Mall
Garden City, NY 11530
Phone: (516) 248-0101
Fax: (516) 248-0132

Trump Palace
1179 Third Avenue
New York, NY 10021
Phone: (212) 639-1101
Fax: (212) 639-1106

King of Prussia Plaza
160 North Gulph Road
King of Prussia, PA 19406
Phone: (610) 992-9144
Fax: (610) 992-9544

Fashion Centre at
Pentagon City
1100 South Hayes Street
Arlington, VA 22202
Phone: (703) 415-5777
Fax: (703) 415-5782

Tyson's Corner Center
1961 Chain Bridge Road
McLean, VA 22102
Phone: (703) 442-8861
Fax: (703) 442-1827

Drew Smith Glasshouse, Inc.
Drew and Kirsi Smith
7793 Bremen Road
Logan, OH 43138
Phone/Fax: (614) 385-2972
e-mail:
smithglass@hockinghill.com

Christopher Farr
Agnes Bourne, Inc.
2 Henry Adams Street
Showroom 220
San Francisco, CA 94103
Phone: (415) 626-6883
Fax: (415) 626-2489

f.kia the Store
558 Tremont Street
Boston, MA 02118
Phone: (617) 357-5553
Fax: (617) 357-5415

studio f.kia
46 Waltham Street
Boston, MA 02118
Phone: 1-800-730-3542 or
(617) 357-5859
Fax: (617) 357-5415

Frederic Williams
200 Lexington Avenue
New York, NY 10016
Phone: (212) 686-6390
Fax: (212) 679-3359

Ground Support Equipment
(US) Ltd.
129 West 22nd Street
New York, NY 10011
Phone: (212) 647-9595
Fax: (212) 647-9596

Henry Gutman
Modern Art & Architecture
508 Chenery Street
San Francisco, CA 94131
Phone/Fax: (415) 239-7063

HAF
79 Grand Street
New York, NY 10013
Phone: (212) 925-3100
Fax: (212) 941-0008

Harry Showroom:
148 South La Brea Avenue
Los Angeles, CA 90036
Phone: (213) 938-3344
Fax: (213) 936-8939

Harry Studio/Warehouse:
8639 Venice Boulevard
Los Angles, CA 90034
Phone: (213) 559-7863

Hastings
Tile/Il Bagno Collection
Kitchen Studio
Corporate Office:
30 Commercial Street
Freeport, NY 11520
Phone: (516) 379-3500
Fax: (516) 379-3187

Hastings showrooms:

230 Park Avenue South
New York, NY 10003
Phone: (212) 674-9700
Fax: (212) 674-8083

404 Northern Boulevard
Great Neck, NY 11021
Phone: (516) 482-11840
Fax: (516) 482-5350

1802 East Jericho Turnpike
Huntington, NY 11743
Phone: (516) 493-1111
Fax: (516) 493-1874

13-100 Merchandise Mart
Chicago, IL 60654
Phone: (312) 527-0565
Fax: (312) 527-2537

Ikeru, Ltd.
466 Washington Street
New York, NY 10013
Phone: (212) 219-3757
Fax: (212) 274-0115

Marjorie Javan Fine Art
85 Newbury Street
Boston, MA 02116
Phone: (617) 556-0040
Fax: (781) 674-9677

Kennedy Studios
140 Tremont Street
Boston, MA 02111
Phone: (617) 542-0868
Fax: (617) 695-0957

Kohler Co.
444 Highland Drive
Kohler, WI 53044
Phone: (414) 457-4441
Fax: (414) 457-6952

Lampa
977 Main Road
Aquebogue, NY 11931
Phone/Fax: (516) 722-9450

Martha Lloyd
c/o Marjorie Javan Fine Art
85 Newbury Street
Boston, MA 02116
Phone: (617) 556-0040
Fax: (781) 674-9677

Mikasa Factory Store
Shoppers World
1 Worcester Place
Framingham, MA 01701
Phone: (508) 620-9503

Phillip Jude Miller
America Dural Interior
Architecture and Design
359 Boylston Street. Ste. 505
Boston, MA 02166
Phone: (617) 267-1699
Fax: (617) 859-5815

Mobelform
1855 Griffin Road
Dania, FL 33004
Phone: 1-888-662-3546 or
(954) 922-7234
Fax: (954) 925-5019

Modern Age
102 Wooster Street
New York, NY 10012
Phone: (212) 966-0669
Fax: (212) 966-4167

Modern Art & Architecture
Henry Gutman
508 Chenery Street
San Francisco, CA 94131
Phone/Fax: (415) 239-7063

Mike Moore
Beverly Furniture
Manufacturing
4859 Gregg Road
Pico Rivera, CA 90660
Phone: (310) 695-5721

On the Fringe
Jacqueline Albanese
Belmont, MA
Phone: (617) 782-2016

Palazzetti Inc.
31 St. James Avenue
Boston, MA 02116
Phone: (617) 482-2335
Fax: (617) 482-2950

Other Palazzetti locations:

9009 Beverly Boulevard
Los Angeles, CA 90048
Phone: (310) 273-2225
Fax: (310) 273-5385

11 Wilton Road
Westport, CT 06880
Phone: (203) 221-3200
Fax: (203) 221-3205

1300 Connecticut
Avenue, N.W.
Washington, DC 20036
Phone: (202) 496-1195
Fax: (202) 496-1194

1001 Northern Bouleard
Manhasset, NY 11030
Phone: (516) 365-7797
Fax: 516-365-8827

515 Madison Avenue
New York, NY 10022
Phone (212) 832-1199
Fax: (212) 832-1385

152 Wooster Street
New York, NY 10012
Phone: (212) 260-8932
Fax: (212) 832-2950

3211 Oaklawn Avenue
Dallas, TX 75219
Phone: (214) 522-1111
Fax: (214) 522-9867

1020 Lawrence Avenue West
Toronto, Canada M6A 1C8
Phone: (416) 785-7190
Fax: (416) 785-7954

Paris Ceramics
A & D Building
150 East 58th Street,
7th Floor
New York, NY 10155
Phone: (212) 644-2782
Fax: (212) 644-2785

Other Paris Ceramics
locations:

8411 Melrose Avenue
West Hollywood, CA 90069
Phone: (213) 653-2230
Fax: (213) 653-2319

151 Greenwich Avenue
Greenwich, CT 06830
Phone: (203) 862-9538
Fax: (203) 629-5484

583 Kings Road
London, England SW6 2EH
Phone: 0171-371-7778
Fax: 0171-371-8395

Christopher Peacock
Showrooms
151 Greenwich Avenue
Greenwich, CT 06830
Phone: (203) 862-9333
Fax: (203) 629-5484

1370 The Merchandise Mart
Chicago, IL 60654
Phone: (312) 321-9500
Fax: (312) 321-9510

1685 Northern Boulevard
Manhasset, NY 11030
Phone: (516) 627-9333
Fax: (516) 627-9474

RC Design
Robert Clisby
7071 Astoria Street
San Diego, CA 92111
Phone/Fax: (619) 277-6644

Nancy Schon
c/o Marjorie Javan Fine Art
85 Newbury Street
Boston, MA 02116
Phone: (617) 556-0040
Fax: (781) 674-9677

Susan Sargent Designs Inc.
Route 30
Pawlet, VT 05761
Phone: 1-800-245-4767
or (802) 325-3466
Fax: (802) 325-6212

Sub Zero Freezer Co., Inc.
Madison, WI 53744-4130
Phone: 1-800-222-7820
or 1-800-444-7820

Sam Tagar
Cambridge, MA
Phone: (617) 497-7297

Translite Systems
1300 Industrial Road, Ste. 22
San Carlos, CA 94070
Phone: (415) 637-8800
Fax: (415) 637-8929

Turnip & Brigs
313 Washington Street
Brookline, MA 02146
Phone: (617) 232-9693

Villeroy & Boch
288 Boylston Street
Boston, MA 02116
Phone: 1-800-575-7442
or (617) 542-7442
Fax: (617) 542-7667

Stephen Whisler Interiors
138 Prince Street
New York, NY 10012
Phone: (212) 431-9302
Fax: (212) 431-7040
Studio Phone:
(212) 343-7967

Frederic Williams
200 Lexington Avenue
New York, NY 10016
Phone: (212) 686-6390
Fax: (212) 679-3359

Zulalian Rug, Inc.
81 Boylston Street
Brookline, MA 02146
Phone: (617) 738-7400
Fax: (617) 738-5268

Acknowledgments

Thank you to a great team: Todd Lyon, a brilliant writer and fantastic artist; Colleen Mohyde, for her considerate and thoughtful presence throughout the evolution of this book; Katie Workman, the senior editor who not only understood the concept of the book, but made it so much more than I could have envisioned it to be, and the entire team at Clarkson Potter; my friend Marcie, to whom I've been reading and calling at 6:00 in the morning for years; Hilda and Mitch, for their encouragement and insights; Jean Yocum, for her inspirational words of wisdom; two great photographers—Steven Randazzo, who captured the essence of the book traveling from home to home with great dignity and talent, and Eric Roth and his team, who amazed us with studio shots that reflect a wonderful creative style; Diane Dubé, the phenominal styling genius who made every shot look great; and all the Domainiacs—Laura Katz and her merchandising team, the warehouse and delivery team, Donna Arruda, Jim McCullagh, Sue Beddia, and Laura Hutchinson.

—Judy George

This book represents three years of rewarding, stimulating, fascinating labor. It was lovingly shepherded from concept to completion by Katie Workman, our miracle-working editor at Clarkson Potter, and Colleen Mohyde, our savvy yet surprisingly sensitive agent.

Many people lent their talents to this project. In addition to the outstanding individuals listed in the credits, we thank all the gifted people at Clarkson Potter, especially Erica Youngren; the great crew at Eric Roth's studio; all the helpful hands at Domain, including Bill Reardon; and Amanda Koster, for her heroic, last-minute camera work.

A mind-boggling number of friends, loved ones, acquaintances, associates and total strangers helped us develop and refine the Intuitive Quiz. We are indebted to all those who participated, especially Lauren Caldwell (and friends), Sandra Shea, Colleen Van Tassell, Kay and Brad Lyon, Cynthia Lyon, Collin Tilton, Barbara Lyon, Steve Maggs, Janet Lyon, Michael Bérubé, Bud Lyon, Sarah Higgins, Susan Manfreda, Cherie and Bob Whaples-Elliot, Jeannie Cavadini, Steven Matzkin, Meg Brazill, Seth Callender, George Baker, Sue Navaretta, John Kehoe, Lynne and Rick Bohan, Lisa Somers, Jack Caldwell, Matthew Holden Lewis, Maria Braëur, Cara Malavolti, Dan Rainville, Shelley Wehrly, JoAnn Coppola, Liz O'Neil, Tom Smith, Pam Haring, Tom McNamara, Tom Hardin (and associates), Jennifer Reiley, Alex DeFelice, Mary McMullen, Wendell Jones, Josh Mamis, Cheryl and David Smyrl, Richard Hulett, Leslie Turnipseed, Anne Donahue, Dawn Mastro, Denise Blake, Jackie Decter, Kim and Jay DiDia, Kris Santella, Mike and Maureen Reichbart, Andrea Rounds, Greta Thomas, Dorie Tilton, the Johnston family, Ben Mazzucco, Glenn Sasse, Sheilagh Mallory, Cat and Bill Holloman, Todd Kutcher, Kathy Evans, Sherri Daley, Paula Treichler, Amanda Anderson, Kevin Terpstra, Larry Brunell, Hugh and Sherri Durham, Marilyn Caldwell, Al Hance, and the many other cheerful participants who, due to our less-than-total recall, are accidentally absent from this list.

Finally, thanks to Hayward Hill Gatling, a cool Idealist with a very Adventurer sense of the absurd and the patience of an Artisan saint.

—Todd Lyon

Credits

Location Photography: Steven Randazzo; Studio Photography: Eric Roth; Location and Studio Styling: Diane Dubé; Additional Photography: Steve Blazo; Additional Styling: Lauren Caldwell; Location Scouting: Janet Henderson for the Eric Roth Studio; Research Assistant: Tamara Alexandra Kruchok

Locations

The following people graciously allowed us to photograph their homes. Their interiors are featured throughout this book. Lisa and Bruce Atkins; Steve Blazo; Rosalie Christiana; Sherri Donghia; Lynn Duff; Steven Finn; Victoria Fitz-Gerald; Lynette "Ned" Hand and Marcello Albanese; Louise Roche-Micciulla and Carmine Micciulla; Joan and Robert Parker; Ursula and Charles Roderick; Lois and Norman Silverman; William Taylor

Many generous individuals allowed us to study their dwellings, as well as their personalities. They are: Tracy Alia and James Vanacore; Judith Altman; Danielle de Benedictus; Beverly Carbonella; Thomasin Desmond; Paula Gold; Alexandria Harvey; Harry Kates; Laurence Lieberman; Larry and Stephanie LiVolsi, Lorenz Studios; Betty Marino; Margaret McKenna; Lisa Riskin

Reference Guide

Page 1: Classic modern table and blown-glass decanter courtesy of Ned Hand and Marcel Albanese. **Page 2:** Roche-Micciulla residence. **Page 6:** Lower left, Podette Swivel Chair from Frederic Williams. Upper left, Creation glass pendant lamp, by Translite Systems. Upper right, inflatable pillow from f.kia the Store. Lower right, urn by Domain. **Page 7:** The Montalembert chair by Mike Moore, from Beverly Furniture Manufacturing Co. **Page 8:** Left, Terrace Bedding from Susan Sargent Designs Inc. Right, Fitz-Gerald residence. **Page 9:** Dining table (1956) by Eero Saarinen, from Palazzetti/Boston. Purple mohair chairs by Barcelona, from Palazzetti/ Boston. Painting by Martha Lloyd from Marjorie Javan Fine Art. **Page 10:** Upper right, Roche-Micciulla residence. Lower left, Domain. **Page 11:** Roche-Micciulla residence. **Page 20–21:** Chanteclaire sofa from Domain. **Page 22:** Upper left, Chanteclaire sofa, silver leaf table lamps, wall sconces, candlesticks, decorative pillows, and throw, all from Domain. *Jeune Homme* by Flandrin, framed print from Kennedy Studios. Leather humidor from Turnip & Brigs. Isepahan Persian rug #842, from Zulalian Rug, Inc. Crystal vases and crystal and porcelain covered boxes from Villeroy & Boch. Lower left, Chanteclaire sofa, end table, ottoman, and throw, all from Domain. Painted frames, miniature chairs, and miniature hat boxes, all from Villeroy & Boch. Stuffed bear from f.kia the Store. **Page 23:** Upper right, Chanteclaire sofa (without slipcover) by Domain. Side table (1932) by Pierre Chareau, from Palazzetti/Boston. *The Seer* by Gottlieb, framed print from Kennedy Studios. Architectural sculpture by Sam Tagar. Art Lamp by Sidney R. Hutter. Lower right, Chanteclaire sofa and folding wicker and iron chair from Domain. Blown vases, platter, and rope and iron lamp, from f.kia the Store. *Body Builder* painting by Todd Lyon. Shirvan Kiliem rug #80 from Zulalian Rug, Inc. Golden Egyptian pillow by Sandra Shea. **Page 24–25:** Antique gold-leaf painting on wood, and cobalt and lead urn, both courtesy of Brad and Kay Lyon. **Page 27:** Silverman residence. **Page 28:** Silverman residence. **Page 29:** Duff residence. **Page 30:** Silverman residence. **Page 31:** Upper left, Atkins residence. Lower right, Duff residence. **Page 32:** Roderick residence. **Page 35:** Roderick residence. **Page 36:** Lamp from Domain. **Page 37:** Tapestry pillows and Elizabeth slipper chair from Domain.

Page 38: Table and chairs from Domain. **Page 39:** Lower left, Silverman residence. Upper right, Washable Posh sofa and cocktail table from Domain. **Page 40:** Lower left, Silverman residence. **Page 41:** Upper left, Atkins residence. Middle right, Parker residence. **Page 42:** Upper left, Roderick residence. Lower right, table from Domain. **Page 43:** Sofa, pillows and throw from Domain. **Page 47:** Parker residence. **Page 48:** Parker residence. **Page 49:** Atkins residence. **Page 51:** Fitz-Gerald residence. **Page 52:** Roche-Micciulla residence. **Page 53:** Parker residence. **Page 54:** Duff residence. **Page 55:** Parker residence. **Page 56:** Lower right, Atkins residence. **Page 57:** Upper right, shardware by Lauren Caldwell. Middle right, Mettowee area rug from Susan Sargent Designs Inc. **Page 58:** Upper left, Roche-Micciulla residence. Lower right, Fitz-Gerald residence. **Page 59:** Fitz-Gerald residence. **Page 60:** Parker residence. **Page 61:** Roche-Micciulla residence. **Page 65:** Finn residence, designed by Phillip Jude Miller for America Dural Interior Architecture and Design. **Page 68:** Christiana residence, designed by Phillip Jude Miller for America Dural Interior Architecture and Design. **Page 69:** Tiled room, courtesy of Paris Ceramics. **Page 70:** Finn residence, designed by Phillip Jude Miller for America Dural. **Page 71:** Duff residence. **Page 73:** Finn residence, designed by Phillip Jude Miller for America Dural Interior Architecture and Design. Painting by Martha Lloyd from Marjorie Javan Fine Art. **Page 74:** Amoeba table by Henry Gutman, for Modern Art & Architecture. **Page 75:** Upper left, match holder from studio f.kia. Upper right, Barcola book table from Directions Contract and Residential Furnishings. Lower right, corkscrew from studio f.kia. Lower left, Lord Yo stack chairs from Modern Age. **Page 76:** Modernist family room from Möbelform. **Page 77:** Christiana residence, designed by Phillip Jude Miller for America Dural Interior Architecture and Design. **Page 78:** Hand/Albanese residence. **Page 79:** Booktable by Ted Boerner Furniture Design. **Page 80:** *Viva Las Vegas* fashion plate by Todd Lyon. **Page 83:** Taylor residence. **Page 84:** Roche/Micculla residence. **Page 85:** "Kids Support Parents," Throne, by Drew Smith Glasshouse. **Page 86:** Taylor residence. **Page 87:** Donghia residence. **Page 89:** Donghia residence. **Page 90:** Upper left, Tool Box area rug by Susan Sargent Designs Inc. Bottom center, Tropical Forest table and painted wooden bowl, Ikera Ltd. **Page 91:** Upper left, vintage noise maker, collection of Diane Dubé. Lower left, metal side table from Domain. Upper right, Man/Woman cabinets from RC Design. Lower right, Day of the Dead bride and groom courtesy of Bill Johnston. **Page 92:** Spiral Screen by Stephen Whisler Interiors. **Page 93:** Tribal Bedding by Susan Sargeant Designs Inc. **Page 94:** Hand/Albanese residence. **Page 95:** Noguchi dining table (1954) by Isamu Noguchi; Opera dining chair by Giacamo Passal; Herbst side chair (1930) by Rene Herbst; Serenella side chair by Biagio Cisotti; and Miss Trip side chair by Philippe Starck, all from Palazzetti/Boston. Upholstered dining chair from Domain. **Page 96:** Atkins residence. **Page 97:** Taylor residence. **Page 99:** Sofa, chair, ottoman, and cushions, Washable Posh from Domain. **Page 100:** Gilded mirror frame from Domain. **Page 101:** Roderick residence. **Page 102:** Domain. **Page 103:** Armoire, sofa, chair, and accessories from Domain. **Page 104:** Con F 191 Rug by Christopher Farr for Agnes Bourne, Inc. **Page 105:** Finn residence, designed by Phillip Jude Miller for America Dural. Barcelona chair (1929), Barcelona cocktail table (1930), daybed (1930), all by Mies Van der Rohe; from Palazzetti/Boston. **Page 106:** Left, Organza Collection pillows from Susan Sargeant Designs Inc. Right, straw hat floor lamp from Lampa. **Page 107:** Taylor residence. **Page 108:** Thought and Speech Bubble Headboard by

Steven Whisler Interiors. **Page 110:** Decorative cushions and Victorian-style lamp from Domain. **Page 111:** Roderick residence. **Page 112:** Soho bed, Chateau chest, and Chateau armoire, all from Domain. **Page 113:** Atkins residence. **Page 114:** Upper right, Finn residence designed by Phillip Jude Miller for America Dural. Interior Architecture and Design Lower right, Bookend table by Ted Boerner Furniture Design. **Page 115:** Habu bed from HAF. **Page 116:** Left, inflatable pillow from f.kia the Store. Right, Hand/Albanese residence. **Page 117:** Hand/Albanese residence. **Page 119:** Hand/Albanese residence. **Page 120:** Custom kitchen by Christopher Peacock. **Page 121:** Parker residence. **Page 122:** Parker residence. **Page 123:** Roche/Micculla residence. **Page 124:** Kitchen by Sub Zero Freezer Co., Inc. **Page 125:** Christiana residence, designed by Phillip Jude Miller for America Dural Interior Architecture and Design. **Page 126:** Upper left, Fitz-Gerald residence. Lower right, Chrome Diner series chair by Harry. **Page 127:** Lyon/Gatling residence. **Page 128:** Donghia residence. **Page 130:** Silverman residence. **Page 131:** Upper left, dinnerware, stemware, and flatware from Villeroy & Boch. Lower left, candlestick from Domain. **Page 132:** Left, Parker residence. **Page 133:** Parker residence. **Page 134:** Courtesy of Paris Ceramics. **Page 135:** Upper left, Gastone folding trolley by Antonio Citterio and Oliver Loew, from Palazzetti/Boston; dinnerware, flatware, and barware from Mikasa Factory Store. Far left, plate and flatware from Villeroy & Boch. **Page 136:** Hand/Albanese residence. **Page 138:** Fitz-Gerald residence. **Page 140:** Silverman residence. **Page 141:** Chair, ottoman, and bookcase from Domain. **Page 142:** Upper left, Washable Posh Slipper Chair from Domain. Bottom, Donghia residence. **Page 143:** Roche/Micculla residence. **Page 144:** Podette swivel chair from Frederic Williams. Modernist table and blown-

glass decanter, courtesy of Ned Hand and Marcel Albanese. **Page 145:** Christiana residence, designed by Phillip Jude Miller for America Dural. **Page 146:** Hand/Albanese residence. **Page 147:** Hand/Albanese residence. **Page 148:** Roche/Micculla residence. **Page 150:** Upper left, Silverman residence. **Page 151:** Roderick residence. **Page 152:** Upper right, Roche/Micculla residence. **Page 153:** Donghia residence. **Page 154:** Upper left, Exodesk, Biomorph interactive desk from Ground Support Equipment (US) Ltd. **Page 155:** Hand/Albanese residence. Lamp from studio f.kia. **Page 156:** Lyon/Gatling residence. **Page 157:** Upper right, Speed bookcase by Robert Clisby, from RC Design. **Page 160:** Roche/Micculla residence. **Page 161:** Upper left, Roderick residence. Lower left, Duff residence. **Page 162:** Left, Parker residence. Right, Donghia residence. **Page 163:** Hand/Albanese residence. Resin knobs on wall from Studio f.kia. **Page 164:** Finn residence, designed by Phillip Jude Miller for America Dural Interior Architecture and Design. **Page 165:** Upper right, Olimpia 70 sink from Hastings. Bottom, free-standing mirror from Becker Designed Inc. **Page 166:** Upper right, photograph *Reduce Speed Curves Ahead* by Kenji Toma; hardware by Kohler. Bottom, Single Toothbrush Holder/ Brush Up Metal series from studio f.kia. **Page 167:** Blazo residence. **Page 172–173:** Original window treatments by Jacqueline Albanese for On the Fringe. **Page 174:** Parker residence. **Page 175:** Atkins residence. **Page 176:** Hand/Albanese residence. **Page 177:** Hand/Albanese residence. Magazine rack from studio f.kia. **Page 178:** Silverman residence. **Page 179:** Hand/Albanese residence. **Page 180:** Upper left, Fitz-Gerald residence. Lower right, Pant File Cabinet from Bravo 20. **Page 181:** Finn residence, designed by Phillip Jude Miller for America Dural Interior Architecture and Design. Sella Magna armchair by Leon Krier, from Palazzetti/Boston.

Quote Bibliography

Page 24: Epictetus, *Good Advice,* William Safire & Leonard Safir, eds., Times Books, 1982.

Page 27: George Bernard Shaw, *The Portable Curmudgeon,* Jon Winokur, ed., NAL Books, 1987.

Page 30: Rainer Maria Rilke, *The New International Dictionary of Quotations,* Second Edition, Margaret Miner & Hugh Rawson, eds., Signet Books, 1994.

Page 37: Carmel White Snow, *Webster's II New Riverside Desk Quotations,* James B. Simpson, ed., Houghton Mifflin, 1992.

Page 44: Sister Parish, *Webster's II New Riverside Desk Quotations,* James B. Simpson, ed., Houghton Mifflin, 1992.

Page 47: J.R.R. Tolkien, *Webster's II New Riverside Desk Quotations,* James B. Simpson, ed., Houghton Mifflin, 1992.

Page 50: Meryl Streep, *The Wordsworth Dictionary of Film Quotations,* Tony Crawley, ed., Wordsworth Reference, 1996.

Page 52: Jean Kinkead Martine, *The Love Nest,* from *Thoughts of Home,* Elaine Greene, ed., Hearst Books, 1995.

Page 62: John Dryden, *Good Advice,* William Safire & Leonard Safir, eds., Times Books, 1982.

Page 70: Edmund Burke, *The Oxford Dictionary of Quotations,* Third Edition, Oxford University Press, 1980.

Page 74: Billy Rose, *Webster's II New Riverside Desk Quotations,* James B. Simpson, ed., Houghton Mifflin, 1992.

Page 80: V. S. Pritchett, *Webster's II New Riverside Desk Quotations,* James B. Simpson, ed., Houghton Mifflin, 1992.

Page 84: William Burroughs, *The Birth of the Beat Generation,* Pantheon, 1995.

Page 91: Robert Venturi, *Webster's II New Riverside Desk Quotations,* James B. Simpson, ed., Houghton Mifflin, 1992.

Page 93: John Ruskin, *The Oxford Dictionary of Quotations,* Third Edition, Oxford University Press.

Page 105: Doris Saatchi, Min Hogg, Wendy Harrop & The World of Interiors, *Interiors,* Clarkson Potter, 1988.

Page 115: Le Corbusier, *Webster's II New Riverside Desk Quotations,* James B. Simpson, ed., Houghton Mifflin, 1992.

Page 125: Thomas Jefferson, *The New International Dictionary of Quotations,* Second Edition, Margaret Miner & Hugh Rawson, eds., Signet Books, 1994.

Page 134: Oscar Wilde, *The Dictionary of Humorous Quotations,* Evan Esar, ed., Dorset Press, 1949 (reprint 1989).

Page 136: Julia Child, *The Quotable Woman,* Running Press, 1991.

Page 146: Errol Flynn, *Webster's II New Riverside Desk Quotations,* James B. Simpson, ed., Houghton Mifflin, 1992.

Page 153: Andrew Wyeth, *Webster's II New Riverside Desk Quotations,* James B. Simpson, ed., Houghton Mifflin, 1992.

Page 155: Albert Einstein, *Webster's II New Riverside Desk Quotations,* James B. Simpson, ed., Houghton Mifflin, 1992.

Page 164: James Gorman, *The Man With No Endorphins,* Viking, 1988.

Index